MASTERING ADVERSITY

Unlock the Warrior Within and Turn Your
Biggest Struggles into Your Greatest Gifts

LANCE ESSIHOS

LANDON
HAIL
PRESS

Cover design: Paul Preston and Matthew Howe
Published by Landon Hail Press
Paperback ISBN: 979-8-9863282-5-6
Hardback ISBN: 979-8-9863282-6-3

DISCLAIMER: This book contains the author's experience with psilocybin (mushrooms) and ayahuasca and is not intended to encourage anyone to break the law or attempt to use these substances outside a legally-sanctioned jurisdiction. The author, publisher, and anyone mentioned in this book who is affiliated with the author's above-mentioned experiences disclaim any loss, risk, or liability that is incurred as a result, directly or indirectly, of the contents of this book.

This book is dedicated to my dad, whom we lost suddenly in 2017. I had the honor of writing his eulogy and felt privileged to be able to express what kind of man he was in a few sentences for his friends and family.

He had a heart of gold and would give you the shirt off his back. My dad didn't have the right tools to handle stress, and when adversity hit, it hit him hard. In a way, this book was inspired by him. Even though our relationship was bumpy over the years, he sacrificed a lot to give me a good life as a boy and as a young man. Although I may have disappointed him more times than I can count, I hope the path I have chosen now, the writing of this book, will make up for all the stress caused. Dad, I hope, as you look down on me from wherever you are, you are proud of the man I've become.

My dad was always there for me when I needed him, and the memory of him in my heart drives me forward every day and reminds me that life is precious and can be taken away from us at any time.

I miss you every day, Dad. Love you forever.
Rest in peace.

TABLE OF CONTENTS

FOREWORD 1

INTRODUCTION 3

    Who Should Read This Book? 4

    An Opportunity for Change: The COVID-19
        Aftermath.. 5

    A Life-Changing Formula 6

    How Do We "Master Adversity"? 8

    Becoming a Warrior 10

CHAPTER 1: MY STORY 12

    Missing Home...15

    One of my Greatest Teachers of Adversity 17

    Losing Focus..22

    You Only Live Once.. 27

    Rough Relationships 29

    Australia...30

    A Priceless Experience..32

    Tragedy 34

    The Alcohol Identity 37

    Saying Goodbye... Again 38

    University of Adversity 41

CHAPTER 2: DEFINING ADVERSITY 44

    Focus on Yourself...48

    Gratitude in Darkness...49

CHAPTER 3: THE FOUR ADVERSITY ARCHETYPES....... 51

Adversity Archetype #1: Distractor 53

Adversity Archetype #2: Victim................................ 56

Adversity Archetype #3: Fixer.................................. 58

Adversity Archetype #4: Warrior 61

Energetic Underpinnings.. 66

CHAPTER 4: TRAUMA... 69

Recognizing Subconscious Programming................ 70

Looking Back with Objectivity and Gratitude 71

Unhealthy Coping–Distractor Behaviors in Response
to Trauma...72

The Lessons in Adversity 75

Trauma Responses.. 76

The Wounded Inner Child 76

Theo Fleury.. 79

Erick Godsey 81

Anger: A Secondary Emotion 82

Healing and Trauma.. 86

CHAPTER 5: THE *5 A's*: A FRAMEWORK FOR MASTERING
ADVERSITY 88

The Adversity Antidotes...90

Move Out of the Wounded Cycle, Into the Healing
Cycle 92

CHAPTER 6: STEP #1: AWARENESS 96

"A Rude Awakening"–Embodying the Distractor 97

Presence: The Antidote for the Distractor............. 105

Cultivating Awareness Through Presence 107

The Impact of our Vices 109

Accountability & Awareness.......................................110

The Unraveling of the Mind Loop............................113

Conscious Healing 115

CHAPTER 7: STEP #2: ACCEPTANCE............................118

A Mother's Love 122

Alcohol and Relationships.. 125

The Transformation..127

"Trauma Bonding"—Embodying the Victim............ 129

Ownership: The Antidote for the Victim.................. 132

Healing the Way We Love 135

The Freedom of Accountability 136

Moving Forward Through Ownership 137

Gratitude for What Is 140

CHAPTER 8: STEP #3: ASPIRE 144

Lance, the Shapeshifter...147

The Law of Attraction 153

Imposter Syndrome... 156

What I Learned After Spending Seven Days with Dr.
Joe... 164

CHAPTER 9: STEP #4: ALIGNMENT.............................. 171

What Really Matters 172

Self-Care..176

It's All in Your Control 177

The Power of Intuition 181

A Profound Reminder.. 189

Intuition: The Antidote to the Fixer 191

Balancing Intuition & Logic...........................193

Meditation 194

Breathwork..198

Creativity, Art, & Personal Expression 203

The Discipline of Intuition...........................206

Plant Medicine: Another Pathway for Tapping into your Higher Self......................................207

CHAPTER 10: STEP #5: ALCHEMIZE.............................212

Alchemy in Action...213

A New Perspective: The Warrior & Healing the Self 216

Embodying the Warrior Within....................221

CONCLUSION 231

THANKS 235

ABOUT LANCE ESSIHOS 237

FOREWORD

*"A bend in the road is not the end of the road—
unless you fail to make the turn."*
—Helen Keller

This is not just another motivational self-help book. This book will change your life and allow you to share the best version of yourself with everyone in the world around you.

My longtime friend and colleague, Lance Essihos, set out to blaze a new trail for healing and success, but along the way he found something more. He reached millions, sharing his wisdom on his top-rated podcast, and realized just how many people need guidance to get through adversity. The result isn't just a book about building grit. It's a call to your courage *and* your resilience. It's a call to live a fulfilling and empowered life full of opportunities, even when things don't go as planned. And let's face it—most of the time, they don't!

He has developed a compelling and essential blueprint for harnessing what he calls "the Warrior within" to overcome challenges and turn any struggle into your greatest gifts. In this book, you will learn how to take ownership of your feelings, cultivate gratitude, develop resilience, and grow your grit to fully flourish in life.

Lance writes like he speaks, which means this book will challenge your beliefs, making you laugh and cry and think and feel as it suggests how to become more of who you already are.

While Lance teaches, he also takes us on an emotional rollercoaster ride through the fundamentals of what it takes to create a life where you can turn shame to grace and pain to purpose. He demonstrates how to look internally for answers instead of numbing out or stuffing down your feelings, by sharing his experience, strength, and hope so authentically and vulnerably.

There is no better person or more qualified expert than Lance to teach us how to be in alignment, overcome adversity, and how to live our lives filled with gratitude and grace to reach true success and profound happiness.

If you have ever been controlled by fear, made decisions based on others' needs, felt like you were alone in your struggle, stuck in your pain, or constantly trudging through mud, read this book, and you will master any adversity.

If you are anything like me and have struggled with trauma, pain, addiction, or being a people-pleaser, you won't be able to put this book down.

If you stick with Lance, I think you can walk away from reading this book with a new appreciation for your own power to create the kind of life you want and to appreciate the kind of life you have. You will become an extraordinary thought leader, growth leader, people builder, friend, parent, and spouse.

Read on. Pass it along. I promise you will never be the same!

Amberly Lago, Motivational Speaker
Bestselling Author, *True Grit and Grace*
Top-Rated Podcast Host, *True Grit and Grace*

INTRODUCTION

"And once the storm is over, you won't remember how you made it through, how you managed to survive. You won't even be sure whether the storm is really over. But one thing is certain. When you come out of the storm, you won't be the same person who walked in. That's what this storm's all about."

—Haruki Murakami

Have you suffered loss or grief? Are you experiencing a dilemma around what is going on in the world and your place in it? Are you dealing with negative self-talk? Are you being confronted with stories from the past that no longer serve you in the present moment? Are you struggling in your personal life due to deep trauma rooted in your childhood? Or you were drawn to this book because you are a student of life, seeking the bravery to become and unleash the true Warrior within and to apply courageous Warrior energy to your life?

Whatever you may be going through that inspired you to pick up this book, I want you to know that I see you. It's why I've written this book. I had to go through hell and back to finally realize that adversity is one of my biggest allies. It has shaped me and molded me into a Warrior and put me on a path to fulfillment, enlightenment, and inner peace.

A quick disclaimer before we begin: I don't claim to have all the answers. Anyone who claims to have it all figured out, in my opinion, is full of shit. Mastering adversity is a process; a lifelong process that becomes easier the more life experience we have. The more adversity, the more challenges, the more struggle that we overcome, the more fully we can see the world as it is. I know my own life experience is simply one part of the journey. I may be further ahead than some, but I am way behind others. That doesn't matter.

In this book, I am going to take you through my own personal journey; to show you what I've gone through in my years on this planet. I am going to show you how I have been able to change my life course to overcome adversity and change my perspective on life for the better.

You may agree with me on some things, and on some things you may not. That is perfectly okay. No matter where you are at or what your beliefs are, I truly believe this book can help change your life.

WHO SHOULD READ THIS BOOK?

This book is for the student of life. This book is for somebody who craves personal growth and meaning. This book is for somebody who has a burning desire to become the best they possibly can, who isn't afraid to look into the darkest corners of their life and isn't afraid to face their fears. This book is for the person who wants to tap into their fullest potential and who is eager to be a leader and experience what it truly means to be a Warrior... This book is for someone who has an inner knowing that they are destined for greatness, yet something is blocking them.

This book is for anyone who has been through challenging times and is ready to face their demons head-on. This book is for the person who no longer wants to live in the stories of the past, knowing that these stories hold them back and no longer define them. This book is for someone who is ready to learn, ready to step into what it really means to live a fully empowered life, and ready to put an end to playing the role of a victim of circumstance. It's time to lean into your fears, your trauma, your negative self-talk, and any other adversity you are facing. It's time to look your past straight in the eye.

This book is for someone who has deep inner knowing that they are meant to do something great, but something has been getting in the way; they feel like they have been playing small. This book is for someone who wants a better understanding of themselves and deeper-level awareness of this life.

It doesn't matter where you are right now or whether or not you are massively successful. What matters is that you have an open heart, an open mind, and are willing to continue to learn and grow. What matters is you consider yourself a humble student of life who wants to serve this world in a bigger way, and you know you can.

If you've gotten knocked down over and over again and you seek a new path, this book will help you see these setbacks as massive opportunities for growth. This book will help you realize, every time you encounter resistance or challenge, it's an opportunity to learn and get better. And later on, when you look back at all the struggles you have been through, you will be grateful they all happened as they did.

AN OPPORTUNITY FOR CHANGE: THE COVID-19 AFTERMATH

I believe this book came at the right time. We need Warriors now more than ever, with the current state of our world. The COVID-19 pandemic and its aftermath have brought adversity to all of us. It has shone a light on our lives and how we show up in all areas. It forced us to slow down and reevaluate our beliefs and priorities. This pandemic showed us where the holes in society are across the board, and it has also given us an opportunity to fix them.

The pandemic has brought a lot of fear, chaos, confusion, and uncertainty to the world, which has led to a steady rise in domestic violence and mental health issues, including suicide. In the midst of this fear, however, there are those who have demonstrated remarkable courage.

My hope is that this book can be used as a tool to help you take your power back. We all have it within in us to be great, but sometimes we forget. I want to help you remember how powerful you really are and how much your life matters. Living a fully empowered life will serve not only you but everyone around you, by giving others permission to do the same.

A LIFE-CHANGING FORMULA

I'm no different than you. I just had a burning desire to make a change when I was in a very dark place. My life was going in a direction that wasn't serving my soul, and one fateful day, I decided to commit to changing my life into one that honored what I knew to be true and to create a life that positively impacts not only myself but the world.

I always had aspirations to make change in the world, but I played small. I listened to the stories I told myself; I thought in a very fixed, scarce mindset. I used to think people were out to get me. I used to think I wasn't smart enough, I wasn't educated enough, I didn't have enough money. I used to tell myself all the excuses in the book.

What I'm going to show you is a formula that has completely changed my life, and I'm confident, by reading this, you are going to be able to use my stories and take the steps I took to make changes in your own life. I went from being a broke bartender to a successful podcaster and entrepreneur—a career that has given me more agency over my life than ever before. Even more importantly, I have been able to heal myself from the trauma and the stories that limited me for so long.

The success I've created, what I've accomplished in the physical realm, doesn't matter as much as the healing I've given my body and mind so I can look at life differently. Now, I can have a general optimism for life and experience more joy and love—things I didn't feel in the past. Through the process of growth, learning, and healing, I have overcome adversity and been able to cultivate love and wholeness within myself, which has allowed me to be able to create this book I am sharing with you.

You see, we don't talk about the end goal that we achieved, when telling our stories. We don't talk about the fancy boats, cars, and houses. When we talk about our journeys, we talk about the shit we went through to get there, because overcoming those things along the way is what actually brings fulfillment in our lives, not the goal, itself, that we achieve. If you don't go through any adversity along your life journey, what kind of story will you tell? By the end of this book, when adversity hits, I want you to be not only ready but *grateful*, because it's an opportunity to grow and level up your life. You'll know, on the other side of the discomfort is fulfillment and an opportunity to share your story with someone else who needs to hear it.

HOW DO WE "MASTER ADVERSITY"?

First of all, mastering anything takes a long time. The reason I called this book *Mastering Adversity* as opposed to *Master Adversity* is that you will never fully conquer it. That is not a guarantee I can make; in fact, I can guarantee you will never fully master adversity. It will always impact you. But the process is still a worthwhile pursuit, and here's why.

If you continue to seek growth and expansion in your life, you will always be faced with a new challenge that will force you to level up. If you aren't being challenged, then you aren't seeking growth or expansion. But when you master challenges or adversity, what will happen is your perspective will change, and the adversity will become easier to get through. No matter who you are, there will always be times that test you and force you to dig deep. If your goal is to have an easy life and you don't want to grow or overcome obstacles, then sure, you'll experience less adversity overall. However, if your goal is to push yourself to the limits and live a fully purpose-filled and empowered life, then I encourage you to get ready and embrace the discomfort that adversity brings. Remember that on the other side of the struggle and the unknown is the treasure you seek.

Mastering adversity is learning to master ourselves and the stories we tell ourselves, which almost always stem from the past; they get in the way of the beautiful present moment and many fresh opportunities. I want to help you step out of the illusion of the past, step into the unknown of the future, and learn to trust the process. When we can stop living in the past and letting the past define our future through a foggy lens, then we can start to create new stories with a clear, fresh canvas every single day. How we look at adversity, or anything in front of us, for that matter, will determine the life experience we have. I want you to realize you have a choice as to what part you will choose.

This book will help you realize that your perspective is literally everything, and the state of your mindset will determine the life experience you have. You will also realize that the biggest changes in your life come from the simple, consistent, daily habits. These compound over time and become who you are. The daily habits create confidence, which creates a stronger level of belief in whatever it is you do. When you have a deeper level of confidence and belief, the challenge in front of you never looks as daunting.

Sometimes, we are looking for the big answers to fall out of the sky, but the reality of it is, how you navigate life all comes down to the daily habits and the daily disciplines. When your daily habits align with your intentions and goals, everything that shows up will feel easier and will bring the success you seek that much faster. When we know we are out of alignment and not doing the things we know align with our truth, then things will feel more challenging than they need to. You will get better at saying no to anything that doesn't bring you close to your goals, and yes to only things that do.

The leaders and spiritual teachers I have admired all allude to our ignorance in the scheme of the Universe. We are all humble students of life. The deeper you go and the more you learn, the more you realize you know nothing of the big picture. Just accepting that is a liberating feeling and takes the pressure off of having to *get* somewhere in some sort of time frame that someone else put in place. Just knowing that there is no finish line and we don't always need to *get* somewhere, and being okay with the present moment and everything it brings, makes life so much more enjoyable.

BECOMING A WARRIOR

The Warrior is a fundamental concept in this book. Embodying the Warrior in our lives is what we are constantly progressing toward when it comes to mastering adversity. I want to take some time to explain this archetype and the concept before we dive into the book, in order to eliminate any misconceptions you might have about the word and encourage you to open up your mind and your heart to new possibilities.

Becoming a Warrior is about rediscovering our deepest truth and learning how to overcome ourselves, every single day. The true warrior essence runs very deep in our ancestral lineage. The fact that you are alive today means someone in your family had to survive some difficult times; in fact, many someones, over many generations. Your ancestors had to survive wars, famine, and many periods of darkness. They had to trust the unknown. It's possible they had to be brave enough to hop on a boat and leave their country to seek a better life. So, if you really think back and really understand that your ancestors sacrificed so much for you to be here right now, my hope is it will help you to realize your true Warrior spirit within you. It has always been there. We all have the Warrior spirit, and this book will help you unlock it and show you how to embody it in all areas of your life.

People have misconceptions around the concept of Warrior because of the movies and other media. They think of the Warrior as this negative, aggressive, bloodthirsty character who seeks conflict and thrives on the battlefield. Yes, this can be a very essential and necessary part of the Warrior archetype, if that time comes to defend your family and what is yours, but it is only one aspect—the shadow side of the Warrior.

A true Warrior comes from a place of love. The Warrior is patient, disciplined, true, and purposeful. He, or she, is brave, courageous, and humble. The Warrior doesn't fear the unknown; they trust that the outcome will serve them or the people they care about. They are willing to die on the sword if they need to, but only if they absolutely must.

Now, of course, we live in different times, and you won't necessarily have to die on the sword or be faced with that choice! However, you will have to fight. You will have to dig deep and find in yourself what it truly means in your life to be a Warrior. The times have changed, the world has changed, but this archetype is still as relevant today as it was a thousand years ago.

It's time for us to step out of the back seat of our lives and into the driver's seat of empowerment. As you discover and home in on the truth about what a Warrior is to you, you will get better at mastering adversity. What that really means is mastering our minds and ourselves. Everyone's life journey is different, but the truth is the characteristics of the true Warrior ethos will be able to serve you in your life, no matter where you're at.

CHAPTER 1

MY STORY

"Opportunities to find deeper powers within ourselves come when life seems most challenging."
–Joseph Campbell

When I think back on my life to determine the most significant experience of adversity I ever went through, it really depends on which lens I'm looking through, because, over the course of my journey, I have grown, healed, and changed alongside these experiences. The different challenges I have overcome have impacted me in different ways. If I had to think back to a moment in my life that affected me the most emotionally–the adverse experience that left me feeling sick and with a sadness I had never experienced before– it was leaving my mother and my big, loving family I had grown up with, when I had to move across the country with my dad.

I didn't know why my parents split up, and because of this, I experienced a lot of inner conflict as a young child. I think parents don't explain these things to their children because they think kids can't handle the truth at a young age; or maybe it's the parent who can't handle the truth. I remember always feeling like I was caught in the middle, and that was a really uncomfortable position.

This part of my life was when the adversity I experienced truly started.

I never realized, when I said "yes" to moving with my father, how much pain, sadness, loneliness, and heartbreak I was about to face. This tight-knit family dynamic had given me so much love up until the age of eleven, when I decided to move away with my dad. I had grown up with such a close, nurturing family—aunts, uncles, cousins, grandparents, all of them—and when I look back at my life, I realize the only reason I am able to have love in my heart and an ability to do what I do today is because of the love I received at such a young age from everybody in my family.

My parents did the very best they could. My dad did everything possible to put food on the table for us. We didn't have a lot, but we had enough to get by. My dad would work late at his graveyard shifts, so my brother and I could play hockey, a very expensive sport. My mom looked after us whenever we needed her.

There was a lot of financial and emotional stress in the family, due to what both of my parents had gone through in their own upbringing. They had been through their own challenges, as children, growing up in unhealthy situations where they didn't learn the tools they needed to start a marriage and have a family.

My parents often fought, trying to work through their differences. When they fought, I remember feeling so scared and anxious. I experienced these supercharged emotions. My nervous system would go into a frenzy, and I would become really dysregulated. But then, I also remember how great it was when they got along. They were just doing their best. When I think back on the love I received from my parents when I was a kid, I am so grateful.

I also think back to the fact that I spent so many of my teenage years rebelling and lashing out at my mom. I was resentful about the marriage ending. I was upset with my mom for leaving and upset with my dad for how he'd treated her. I think back to those times and realize I just felt lost and scared. The only way I knew how to process my feeling of resentment was through anger, and I really was an asshole to both my parents for many years. I would freak out and call them names. Some of the fights we had were pretty wild, especially with my dad. A few times, the cops were called on us because of the screaming.

When I went to visit my mom, usually in the summers, we got into some pretty intense fights, too. I think we both got upset and emotional because we knew we would have to say goodbye again at the end of our visit, and we never knew when we would see each other again. Those were some of the hardest moments of my life. I remember this particular challenge being extremely heartbreaking, because each visit—even though it brightened my day when I saw her—reminded me we were no longer together. I felt literally sick for days after saying goodbye.

This process really hardened me, which did serve me in some ways but also made it harder for me to open my heart later in life. The truth is, conflict, fighting, and dysfunction are all we knew. Looking back now, I realize I did the best I could with the challenging situation I was experiencing, and so did my family.

The way we face adversity in our lives all comes back to the stories of the past, of what we have gone through. The future challenges I faced were always highly triggering and emotional, because I had this lingering sense of anxiety that I never understood. It wasn't until later that I realized it was created from the constant stress within my family.

A lot of how we look at life today is based on the timeline of what we went through—both good and bad.

Those years I endured, although very challenging emotionally, were some of the best years of my life, and they established a foundation that some people don't have the opportunity to experience, because they don't even have a family. Even after my parents split up, I was still fortunate enough to be able to see my mom occasionally, and I am thankful for that.

MISSING HOME

My dad's family in Victoria, BC were very loving but also very different, and it was a huge adjustment for me, to say the least. I remember missing my mom so much I would start to feel sick to my stomach when I thought about her. My heart ached, and even long-distance phone calls were an issue back then.

Back then, phone companies charged per minute, so you couldn't just get on the phone and talk for hours like we can now. I always felt the pressure when my mom called or when I called her, and my dad's negative commentary about my mom didn't help. He would tell me she was selfish and that their demise was her fault. "Your mom left us," he would say.

I missed my friends, my school, my local spots, and my community. When I look back, I realize I felt really alone and defeated, although I didn't truly know what I was feeling at the time, because I wasn't even a teenager. I had to completely start over, and the fear began to set in.

I had moved from a school where I was the cool kid and the star athlete. I had participated in some of the best tournaments in the world and played with some of the greatest players, some who ended up making it to the NHL. This new school wasn't what I'd expected, and I didn't fit in. At my old school, I was popular. I had an older brother who was respected, so no one would mess with me. At this new school, I felt like I was a nobody.

It was an inner-city school where kids were skaters. They came from many different backgrounds and different families without a lot of money, a different scene than I was used to. I stood out, and I got bullied. I didn't know how to handle that, because I was so used to being in control and being a dominant figure in how things went in the school yard or in the classroom. It was a real mindfuck for me to be the kid who didn't fit in.

I became the kid who got scissors thrown at his head; the kid who went to the bathroom and had to fight two or three other kids, then pretend like nothing happened when I went back to the classroom, because I didn't want to rat on anybody. The tormenting went on for a while. I went from living in one world, and then, overnight–literally–I was thrust into another. In those challenging moments, my confidence, my belief in myself, and my ability to communicate with others was damaged. And that was just the beginning.

I spent so much time as a kid feeling like something was wrong with me. All I looked forward to was talking to my friends back home on the phone or to my mom. I felt so embarrassed. I felt like a failure. I constantly asked myself, *Why am I not fitting in? What is wrong with me?* As a child, these questions continued to come up in my mind. Even reflecting on this now brings up a lot of emotion.

People don't really realize how much bullying hurts when you're a kid, and not only was I dealing with trying to avoid getting bullied, I didn't really have a home base that was comfortable, either. My dad was working, I was home alone, and there was none of the connection I needed amongst my family members or much understanding of how I was feeling. I always felt isolated, like I was on an island and no one knew I was there. My older brother and my mom were back in Edmonton, and I missed them so much.

Looking back, those six months in seventh grade, in 1995, were some of the most challenging of my life. I can't imagine what it would have been like to have social media and cell phones. I never would have been able to escape! Not having every little thing documented and a million ways to be contacted and bullied back then was such a blessing.

I always hoped for a fresh start the next day. *Maybe they'll forget about what happened yesterday*, I would think, and then try to hide and stay away.

ONE OF MY GREATEST TEACHERS OF ADVERSITY

After six months, I was able to move schools. We moved across the city into a very different area. I finally got the fresh started I needed. I'm so thankful my dad heard me and listened to me, allowing me to feel happy again.

Even with the change, this marked a time that I remember as being especially challenging. My dad met a woman who had four kids. This also marked the first time my intuition spoke to me. I immediately knew she was bad news. I knew that her energy and the way she was coming on to my dad didn't feel right.

My dad and I had just started doing well together, and he was all I had. Financially, things were starting to get a little bit better, and I was getting used to being away from the rest of my family. I was playing competitive hockey, juggling early-morning practices at 5:30 a.m. before school, and was really leaning on my dad.

This woman's son played on my hockey team, and he was a friend of mine, which made things doubly difficult. She began to use the situation of us being teammates and friends to manipulate my dad. She was going after him for stability for her kids and for her family at the expense of our own.

One day, when I was twelve years old, I was really upset with my dad and had an outburst, telling him how I felt about her. Unfortunately, at that same moment, she was coming in the back door and heard everything I said. From that moment on, she had very negative energy toward me, and our relationship was never the same. What hurt the most was that I was never actually heard or acknowledged, and no one wanted to make any effort to mend the relationship.

One summer, when I went away for a couple months to visit family, she convinced my dad to move in with her and her four children. I felt so unsettled, because I knew she didn't have good intentions. Deep down in my gut, I knew she wasn't a good person.

When we all began living together, a lot of crazy shit went down. Things you only see in the movies! She blocked my mom's phone number. She signed for my mail and then discarded it. She got rid of things that came from my family. One time, my mom sent me a holiday card with family photos, and I never received it, so my mom traced the package and saw my stepmother had signed for it but never delivered it to me. When I asked her where the card went, she denied ever seeing it.

I also had my own phone line in the basement, and she blocked my mom's number from calling. She did whatever she could to be a pain in my ass. I just wanted to leave. I even thought of killing myself many times because I couldn't handle the pain, but the thought of hurting any member of my family kept me alive.

This woman made a big scene within the hockey community and acted completely inappropriately. It was embarrassing. She always exuded this energy of victimhood, and it was manipulative. She carried things that were too heavy for her just for attention, just so someone would rush over to help her. She tried to make herself seem like a charity case because she had four children. Her behavior was transparent to me, but she was able to manipulate my dad.

I had so much shame and embarrassment because we were known as the goofy family with no money. We really stood out within the hockey community, and her "poor me" mentality made it more apparent that we weren't the most well off. I was so emotionally messed up not only from getting bullied the year before and being away from my family but also from having to deal with this crazy woman who I knew didn't truly love my dad.

Because of this, I started to act out and turned into a class clown. I felt I could fit in and get approval if I was funny enough and didn't take life too seriously. It helped me escape. Looking back now, it makes a lot of sense, because I didn't have any confidence. I was just doing really stupid things, goofing around and being a teenager. I realized I was seeking approval of some sort because I lacked confidence in myself.

Really, the one thing that kept me going at that time was my hockey career. I was doing well, but there were still issues. There was an emotional strain, because I was friends with my dad's wife's son, who was on the same team, but I wasn't getting along with her or the rest of her family. What made things even more difficult was when she got pregnant with my younger brother. During that time, she used the baby as ammunition and held it against my dad all the time.

I remember her coming into the hockey arena and making a big scene, putting down my dad and accusing him of not being helpful enough or doing enough. She was always a victim. It was such a toxic manipulation of energy that we all had to deal with. For two decades, she tormented my dad and tore our entire family apart.

When my dad split up with her about a year later, she did everything in her power to keep him from seeing my younger brother. She pulled every trick in the book and stirred the pot so bad, he would lose his temper, which led to him being arrested twice and charged with harassment; after that, he could only have supervised visits with my younger brother. All because he wanted to see his son. And when I look back at this, it's hard for me to imagine any father who wouldn't do the same, when faced with her crazy antics.

For family dinners with my little brother, we always had my dad's homemade spaghetti and tomato meat sauce. I clearly remember having to eat with some random supervisor at the table during our visits. This was up there with one of the weirdest situations I've ever experienced. We all had this strange sense of shame and embarrassment, which seemed never-ending.

This was really one of the most ridiculous turns of events I've ever witnessed. My dad's ex-wife was able to manipulate the court system, the judges, and the whole legal apparatus in her favor, as a victim. This really made me distrust the legal system in general—seeing how it could fail so miserably due to someone telling blatant lies.

She was a pathological liar. And nobody could seem to see that. She played the victim and collected sympathy in any area possible, not to mention as much money and child support from my dad as possible. So, because my dad wore his heart on his sleeve and would give anyone the shirt off his back, she worked that in her favor and exploited his good nature, when they were together. She then used his temper against him—he had a temper; there's no denying that. In this case, however, his temper was understandable. She baited him into getting upset, and then he would threaten her, as any man would, if he were put in a similar situation, with his back against the wall.

She would threaten him, keep his child from him, and, at the same time, drain him for every cent he had. It's human nature to get upset. Yes, he didn't do the right thing, at times. And yes, he made mistakes and lost his temper. But she was a master at manipulation, and she had the whole world fooled.

I vividly remember one morning, when I was walking down the stairs of our house on my way to school, I saw my dad's white coffee mug sitting on the sidewalk. I was baffled as to why it was there. Later, I found out he had been arrested and left his cup there. Saying that was a strange feeling would be a complete understatement.

The court determined he was not fit to raise a child, even though he was raising me and my brother successfully. In addition to making it nearly impossible for my dad to see my youngest brother, my dad's wife did whatever she could to take every little bit of money from my dad for child support until my younger brother was eighteen years old, which made life even harder for all of us.

Hockey is a very expensive sport, so that, on top of paying the electric bill and putting food on the table, meant we were just able to get by. Anybody who knew me back then knows, in that house, there wasn't a lot of food in the fridge. I'm definitely not saying we were poor, but every extra cent outside of our family bills went to her. My dad drove the oldest car, which he ended up passing down to me—a 1984 gold Toyota Tercel—and he lived very modestly, just so we could survive.

The reason I tell this story in such detail is because these years caused unimaginable chaos in my family, as well as stress that I believe led to the premature deaths of my father and brother. Now, I'm not blaming her directly for their deaths, but if you'd been there, you would've seen how, for years, every single conversation I had with my family revolved around this woman. At a certain point, my dad started to blame me for driving her out. This was far too much to put on a young man. I know, deep down, he knew it wasn't true, but when he got upset, he couldn't control his emotions, and that's what would come out. He needed someone to blame, so he didn't have to face that the decision he'd made had failed.

Those years really impacted me in a way that left me feeling very alone and very unsafe, mostly because I never felt like I had a good, solid home base. Mix this in with teen years, where you're trying to fit in, trying to make it in sports, meeting girls, and living on not very much money, and it amounts to significant adversity.

LOSING FOCUS

When I look back at my life, so many valuable skills came from all of the years I played sports. There were moments when things were challenging, but they were made up for with moments that were so deeply validating.

When you are a competitive athlete like I was with ice hockey, you have to dedicate your life to it. When you have to commit to something at such a young age that is bigger than yourself, like I did, when you have a goal only a small percentage of people are capable of achieving, the dedication you must have to get to that level of professionalism is very difficult at times. Your team becomes more important than your own individual needs. Your identity becomes wrapped up in your role as an athlete and wrapped up in making it professionally– nothing else matters. If you want to make it professionally as an athlete, it requires persistence in working toward your goals, a strong work ethic, punctuality, dedication, being coachable, checking your ego at the door, and so many other qualities.

I never made it professionally as an athlete because I wasn't dedicated enough. Over the years, because of my emotional instability, I didn't know how to channel my thoughts and my feelings, so the minute that alcohol was introduced into my life, it gave me a sense of freedom. It allowed me to create a new persona for myself that didn't exist before. As I started to dabble with alcohol in my early teens and into my late teens, I lost sight of my goal of wanting to make it as a professional athlete. I was partying and really liked what I was doing. Nearly all teenagers or young adults participate in activities like drinking and partying, but as an athlete, a lot of focus is required to succeed, and I was losing that focus.

At the time, I was playing junior hockey, and I really had the opportunity to go somewhere with it. The problem is, when you're that age, nobody's teaching you what setting intentions means, what that long-term goal-setting really looks like, or how to manage your "work/life balance" to continue taking care of yourself.

After getting traded that summer from the Coquitlam Express to the Langley Hornets of the British Columbia Hockey League, I decided to go and not only party during the offseason but take a big cycle of steroids. I thought, if I could get stronger and quicker in a short period of time, it would give me the edge I needed to get a NCAA scholarship for college.

I took a cycle of Deca and Sustanon, and I gained twenty-five pounds. I got to training camp that summer for my final year in junior hockey at age twenty years old. Basically, this was my last kick at the can to make it anywhere in hockey.

My coach said, "What's wrong with you? Why are you so heavy? You're going to have to lose weight."

I couldn't skate, couldn't move on the ice I was drinking all summer, I wasn't committed, and before you know it, I was released from the Langley Hornets British Columbia Hockey League. Just like that, my Junior A hockey career was over.

Part of me was relieved that it was over; hockey had consumed my life for so long—I hadn't had weekends off like other kids, and at times, I'd longed for a normal existence. When the dust settled and I realized what I had done, however, things started to sting. It was definitely a "grass is greener" mentality; reality—finding a normal job, paying rent, bills, etc.—wasn't all that glamorous. I regretted not trying harder. I finished off the year in Campbell River playing Junior B, but my heart really wasn't in it after playing at a higher level for the two years prior.

That year, and after, I got into some really heavy drinking and drugs—a lot of ecstasy, a lot of things that really fucked up my brain, including ecstasy laced with meth. I literally felt my entire brain change, and within a year, I developed extreme anxiety. My mom warned me that would happen, because she experimented with drugs in her youth and experienced it herself. I always had an underlying feeling of anxiousness in social situations, but I didn't understand what real anxiety was until this point in my life.

As a teenager and young adult, I was able to smoke marijuana, but I remember smoking after this year of heavy drug use and having a panic attack. I feel like I've been traumatized ever since. I remember smoking and then feeling this feeling like my heart was going to come out of my chest. I was sitting in my room and suddenly felt like I was blacking out. I felt dizzy and like I was going to faint. I was sweating and thought I was dying. That feeling has stuck in my brain ever since then. Anytime I do any sort of plant medicine or anything along those lines, I wonder if I am going to have that experience again. I know it came from doing hard drugs and messing with my brain chemistry.

The anxiety I developed made me paranoid, and that feeling caused me to spiral into this world of needing to drink all the time. I was trying to find my way after hockey, which was very tough as it was, but at the same time, I was dealing with this chemical imbalance from doing drugs and drinking. I went through some really dark times after leaving my identity behind. It was hard to explain to family, friends, and really everybody who knew me why I'd failed as a hockey player.

I didn't have the tools to move forward in life, because hockey was all I'd ever done or known. When you're an athlete, you're so laser-focused on being an athlete, you don't really think about anything else. So, you create this identity, and you become that. When that ends, however, you don't know who you are. There's a sense of letting go and the death of that persona or former self. For me, it was very hard, because that's all I knew. So, moving forward, I asked myself, "Who am I going to be after sports? Who am I going to be after basically taking my own career and flushing it down the toilet?" I didn't have the answers.

As I look back now, I know I did the best I could with what I knew, but the choices I made still linger in my mind. Young people just want to be accepted, heard, and loved. I felt so lost, so sad, and so depressed. I missed my family, and I didn't know what I was going to do with my life. I tried working as a laborer in many different trades, but that didn't honor who I was. I'm a people person, and I needed to get into an environment that allowed me to shine as a human being.

I explored many different careers. I was a vending machine guy and worked nights for Coca-Cola in the warehouse (one of the worst jobs I've ever worked). I did sales and retail, too. At the time, I was trying to become a cop, but that didn't work out. Then, I wanted to become a firefighter. I did my pre-paramedics, but I ended up failing my practical course. I was doing it just for the glamor of it; I thought it would be cool to be a firefighter because all my other hockey buddies were doing it.

Then, I tried my hand in the bar and restaurant industry. I remember getting my first job doing room service at the Marriott, which gave me a taste of something new, and then at The Keg in Victoria. On my first shift as a busser, I right away liked the feeling of working in a restaurant—hustling, getting glasses, being around beautiful women, and being rewarded with tips at the end of the night. I remember thinking, *This is the life*. And that's where the bar journey started and where a huge chunk of my life was invented.

To me, the bar and restaurant industry was magnetic. I was able to have fun, be around people, make friends, meet women, make money, and there was lots of alcohol to drink. It was almost as if the bar industry was satisfying all the areas of my life that I enjoyed. I had some of the wildest, craziest experiences.

This industry felt like a rockstar lifestyle to me and the next best thing to playing sports. When you're an athlete and you play at a high level, you get all the things and all the attention. You get to be around people, and you feel like you're somebody. In the bar and restaurant industry, I noticed I was rewarded for the things I was good at. I was compensated nightly for a job well done. I was paid handsomely in tips for working hard, building relationships with people, being energetic, having fun, flirting with the ladies, and being able to hide in this weird world of toxic chaos.

YOU ONLY LIVE ONCE...

I started off as a busser in a restaurant and worked in a hotel, doing room service at age twenty-two. Then, at twenty-three, I moved to Vancouver, BC, with a woman I was dating. There, I ended up working at one of the hottest restaurants in the city as a server. She introduced me to the general manager, who ended up hiring me.

I was so broke at the time, I could only afford one set of work clothes—a white dress shirt, black pants, a purple tie, and black shoes. I had to sell my TV to make rent. Luckily, my girlfriend's family was awesome, and they helped me get all the essentials, like plates, bowls, knives, forks, etc., from IKEA. They really helped me with my transition, and I am forever ever grateful for that.

Starting out fresh and in a new city was tough but so worth it. When I started at the restaurant, I was still really new in the industry, so for me, it was the coolest thing ever. I was surrounded by the most beautiful women, I was making great money living in a beautiful city, and my life was pretty incredible. But what I didn't realize was that I was diving into an industry where I could hide. I could hide behind alcohol, I could hide behind the partying, and I could escape myself.

At the time, I didn't realize that's what I was doing. There were a lot of deep-rooted emotions, a lot of deep-rooted problems I was running from, that showed up in all the relationships I had. Don't get me wrong: these were some of my wildest times, and it was the most fun I ever had, but it was also really challenging.

I would drink to the point of getting a bad hangover, and subsequently, I would get really depressed. I knew what I was doing didn't feel right, but I also wanted to live that "you only live once" mentality. It was an internal battle for years.

Bartending was something I got into within a year after I started in the service industry, and it was something I was really good at. It was the first time something got me really excited. It ticked all the boxes; it allowed me to be this person whom I could hide behind. It was essentially like creating a new person.

You get rewarded for putting on parties and for being the party guy. I enjoyed serving my guests. I enjoyed making drinks. I enjoyed all of this action. There's a certain level of importance you have when you play sports in front of a crowd. You're somebody. When I was behind the bar, I felt like I was somebody, too. There was a rush to the busyness of it. Making drinks, taking shots. Then, after my shift, I was able to go out and have beers with the team or go to a party. It was all the things I wanted, but I didn't have to play a sport and feel the pressure of playing sports to enjoy it. It was a really crazy time, and for the next decade or more, I worked in every single environment in the bar industry you can imagine, from restaurants to pubs to casinos to nightclubs and private parties—you name it, I worked it.

The problem when you're in that industry is you start to get really deep into it, and your life becomes a big party. It was a wild, crazy, fun ride, but it begins to take over your life. I started to become addicted to escaping. I loved going out and getting fucked up with all my friends whenever I could, because it felt like I could escape my reality—the pain of my home life as an adolescent and of missing my family, whom I wasn't in touch with.

There were times when I wouldn't take a day off, drinking for weeks at a time, taking shot after shot. I would drink a shot the morning after a night of drinking, then more shots at work. It just never ended. I was going back and forth in this loop of getting fucked up, then doing damage control—whether it was sweating it out, marijuana, coffee to get back to work, a nap, etc. Existing in this state never allowed me the opportunity to build on anything; it was like I was on a hamster wheel.

I started to use drugs more frequently, which made things a lot more difficult. When you start to associate with people who are doing more drugs, you start to do more drugs, and that becomes part of your life, too. There was a period there when I was doing a lot of cocaine and a lot of MDMA mixed with alcohol. It was not a recipe for a productive life. I look back at how I treated my body and how I felt in general... I was really struggling.

I struggled with so much, even with daily life. I was trying to be a good person and trying to follow a path, figuring out what I wanted to do. I attempted to go to college and study marketing, but because I was working so much, I couldn't handle the course load, and I flunked out. I felt my only option at that time was bartending, and I embraced it. I partied for a living.

ROUGH RELATIONSHIPS

In my early twenties, I was in a relationship that was off and on for about three years. Looking back, I can remember how much of an emotional basket case I was. I was still dealing with all the family stuff from back home on top of dealing with my own personal shit—ironically, my personal shit stemmed from everything I'd experienced as a child and that I was trying to escape with my vices.

All of my relationships in my twenties had the same thing in common: I had this little-boy energy, this abandonment energy, along with inner conflict. When I drank, my temper would get out of control, and I said things that hurt my girlfriends. My actions when I was drinking brought about the demise of most of my relationships. When I was sober for a while, my anxiety and relationship dysfunction went away, but then I would fall back into it. I experienced a challenging dance with alcohol for the duration of my twenties.

I was in a relationship when I was twenty-eight and twenty-nine, and things got really bad. It wasn't either of our fault; we weren't healthy for each other. We were both going through our own traumas and processing life, and it was really challenging. So, when I was twenty-nine years old, after that relationship ended, I decided to sell everything I owned and move to Australia.

I could feel myself going down a road that I wasn't proud of, hanging around with people and doing things I knew weren't going to serve me later in life. I just knew, if I continued on this way, it wasn't going to end well. So, in December 2012, I sold everything, bought a one-way ticket to Australia, and took off for my new life.

AUSTRALIA

I didn't think I would stay in Australia long term, but I ended up living there for five years. My initial plan was to get out of the bar industry and into something else. I really wanted to see what else I could do in a different country other than just pour drinks.

But when we are comfortable with something and we're good at it, and when it allows us to be able to connect with people and meet people, it's natural to jump right back into it, which is exactly what I did. I was fortunate enough to work at some great bars—some of the best bars in Australia, from the Gold Coast to Port Douglas in Northern Australia, and then eventually Sydney, which became my home for three years. I managed to get a sponsorship, where I worked for one of the best hotel and bar companies in Australia. These were some of the greatest times of my life. I got to meet so many amazing people and build so many great relationships, but I also pushed my body to the absolute max; there was a point where I thought I would possibly die.

The Australian party scene is pretty intense. Sunday sessions are like a religious ritual, and everybody gets together and drinks. These sessions usually last late into the night and sometimes into the morning. Working in the bar industry in Australia wasn't just a job; it was a lifestyle. People like to have fun. People like to party. Trying to escape that lifestyle in an environment surrounded by constant partying subconsciously drew me toward it that much more.

There was a time when I would go to work on a Thursday, starting at 3:00 p.m., and then go out drinking all night, come back in the morning, sleep for a few hours, go back to work at 3:00 p.m. on Friday, drink three or four shots of vodka and three or four shots of espresso, and start my day. Sometimes, I would look back on my Thursdays, Fridays, and Saturdays, and it was just a blur. I was just barely holding on to stay afloat.

We'd go to the Smoking Panda in the Sydney CBD after work. It was the hot spot for people working in the bars, because it was one of the only bars that stayed open late. It was absolute insanity in this place. We'd get in around 3:00 a.m. for drinks and stay until about 6:00 in the morning, and as soon as the cocktail bar closed, we went down to the pub to drink and do whatever drugs were around until 10:00 in the morning, when we'd hit up McDonald's, get $50-$60-worth of food, and then I'd hop in a $30 Uber back to where I lived in Bondi Beach. Absolute insanity.

These were some crazy, wild times. I can look back and laugh about it now, but I also think about what I put my body through and just how insane my thought process was. The fact that I was able to hold a job during all this baffles me. 2014 through 2016 was a wild ride of partying and working—*wash, rinse, repeat.*

A PRICELESS EXPERIENCE

In 2015, at the very end of the year, my dad decided to come visit me in Australia. It was great to see him for the first time in three years. I hadn't seen him since I left in December 2012. There was distance between us after what had happened with his ex-wife, and being in different time zones, we just didn't talk as much. Because the flight from Australia to Canada is so expensive and because it was difficult to take a lot of time off, it was challenging for me to come back and visit Canada. And to be honest, I wasn't in a big hurry to go back and visit. I was happy to be away.

It had started to look like Australia was going to be my home base, because I loved the culture and the beach life. People there know how to enjoy life, they know how to have fun, they know how to be healthy—the whole package. The all-around lifestyle of Australia was really attractive to me. I was surrounded by a lot of beautiful women, having a lot of great conversations, and making pretty good money at the time. Life was pretty good, other than the occasional feeling of emptiness I would experience. Despite that, I had accepted that bartending and bar management was my career of choice; the path I was going to take, in hopes that it would develop into some further career path within the hospitality industry.

When my dad came to visit, we spent a lot of time together. Since there was such a divide between us over the years when I was a teenager and because of the trouble caused by his ex-wife, we had lost our level of closeness. So, when we got together after years, we really got to rekindle the bond we had had when I was younger.

It was challenging, too, though. He stayed with me for six weeks in a tiny 500-square-foot, 1970s bachelor pad. We almost killed each other in it a couple times. It was small and very hot. He slept on the couch, while my mattress was on the floor behind the couch. We had zero privacy.

The apartment was located on the street level on one of the busiest streets in Bondi Beach, next to a bus stop, so there was a continuous flow of people walking by. I had no blinds, only curtains, so it was either open up the sliding window and curtains to have the world look in or keep the curtains and window closed and bake in the heat. We had two noisy fans blowing all the time to cool us off. The blazing summer 97-degree Australia heat created a lot of friction and discomfort. Despite that, being able to spend that much time with him was pretty special. I couldn't remember the last time I'd been able to do that, and even though I didn't know it at the time, it would be the last time I would be able to spend that much time with him.

We brought in 2016 together and got to see Christmas in Australia on Bondi Beach. The experience was like something out of a dream. Imagine people from all over the world wearing Santa hats, drinking on the beach, dance parties, and having picnics and barbecues. It's really just an amazing experience, and it's completely different from anything you could imagine in North America for Christmas. It's about being social; it's about getting together and having fun. It's the opposite of the consumerist approach to the holidays I was used to.

It was priceless to see my dad experience this, because he'd never been part of something like it before.

TRAGEDY

The beginning of 2016 was when things really started to change.

I went back to work at the very beginning of January, while my dad stayed in my apartment. At the time, I think he was watching tennis, as it was right in the middle of the Australian Open. He also had an iPad to keep himself occupied. We didn't have cable TV or anything like that, but he was content enough just hang to out while I was at work

I was at work when my older brother texted me, telling me to call him. I got on the phone, and he gave me the news. He told me that our younger brother had taken his own life. My older brother had received a call from one of my ex-stepbrothers. He was also contacted by the police, so it was confirmed true.

At that moment, I went into complete shock. I didn't know what to think, because I had never experienced anything this devastating in my life.

This isn't something that happens to our family... to me... This only happens in the movies... Right? How am I going to tell my dad this?

I felt sick to my stomach. I felt terrified. I didn't know how he was going to react. I also felt so much guilt. My dad was a very emotional person, and he didn't deal with stress very well, which, later on, in my opinion, led to his premature passing.

I told my coworkers I had to go and called my boss. The team did really well and just took over without me. They gave me amazing support, telling me to take all the time that I needed.

I found myself sitting frozen in the Uber, thinking, *What the fuck am I going to tell my dad? This is just brutal. He's going to be so devastated.*

So many different scenarios played out in my head. A deep, sick feeling in the pit of my stomach took over my body. Those minutes I spent in the Uber were some of the most surreal minutes of my life.

How am I going to tell my dad that his son died... Not only that he died, but that he killed himself?

I thought about what must have been in his head to drive him to make that decision and how much pain he must have been in. I felt so much guilt and regret about how I could have helped him.

When I got home, I told my dad there was some really bad news. I looked him in the eyes, and he looked back at me with an expression of innocence, waiting for my words. He asked me what was going on.

I wasn't really sure what to say. It went something like, "Look, somebody has taken their own life, and you know it's not good." He started to guess different people in our family, frantic and panicked. I knew that this information would destroy him, but I had no choice but to tell him it was, in fact, my younger brother, his son.

The color left his face. I'll never forget that moment and the feeling in that room of my small, dingy bachelor pad. It was dark, and he was sitting by the one window in the room when I told him the news. His face and his whole body shifted into this sick feeling.

I don't really remember what happened after that, but a few hours later, we ended up going for a run together to relieve some of the stress. Then, we did a workout outside, because it was the only thing we really could do. There are these outdoor gyms in Sydney on Bondi Beach where you can go do pull-ups and dips, and that's what we did to break through the stress and terror of our current reality. The next step was planning our trip back to Berry to say our goodbyes. My dad's trip was cut short.

From that moment on, life would change forever. Things were never going to be the same. Losing a family member like that is something you never think will happen to you. We didn't understand how to take what had just happened and move forward.

When my little brother was a teenager, I remember thinking to myself, *When he turns eighteen, I'm going to make an effort to reconnect with him and explain my story around the whole family situation—the nightmare situation we have been in since he was born.* I felt, when he was that age, it would be the right time to have that conversation. But unfortunately, that conversation never happened. We lost him two months before his nineteenth birthday.

When something like this happens to somebody in your family, you immediately try to figure out how you could have done things differently; how you could have fixed it; where you could have shown up better. I had so much deep guilt in my heart. I felt like I hadn't been there for him when he needed me. But it was always such a difficult situation, because his mother got in the way of any of us having a real, healthy relationship with him. She interfered in all of our conversations over the years, and I just grew really tired of all the bullshit. That was a huge reason why I moved away to Australia in the first place. I didn't want to deal with the drama anymore, so the sacrifice I'd had to make was to disconnect myself from him.

Thinking about not getting that opportunity to reconnect with him still hurts to this day, because, even now, I know I could have saved his life. I look at the work I've done with my podcast and I just know I could have been a forever resource to help him out. But I also know now, with the lens of life I look through today, that I did the best I could with what I had.

THE ALCOHOL IDENTITY

The shame I felt over this for the rest of 2016 sent me into a downward spiral. All I did was drink and work in order to push the event out of my mind. I worked ten- to twelve-hour days, five days a week, and sometimes, six. During my shifts, I drank like crazy, punishing my body, and I stayed up late. I did have some fun, but it was very taxing on my body.

Some nights, when I got home, I would lie on my bed in a pool of sweat, because I had such anxiety I couldn't sleep. I was so tired, but I would wake up in the middle of night with tremors. I was asleep, and then, suddenly, I would jump up, freak out, and then realize it was nothing and go back to sleep. I can't imagine what I was doing to my nervous system. I would lie there in this anxiety, and sometimes the only way to take care of it and to calm my nervous system was to have another drink.

There was a time when I couldn't fly on airplanes without alcohol. I couldn't go out to eat without alcohol. I couldn't socialize without alcohol. It became a part of my identity.

At the time, I had a girlfriend, whom I ended up being with for three years. Now, she is married and has a child, but I look back and feel as though it was such a blessing that I met her, because she gave me a reason to want to get out of that shit. Meeting her was an essential part of my journey. She helped me through some tough feelings and some late nights, and to this day, I don't know why she put up with that stuff when she did, because I was an absolute nightmare for the first six months after we met, in 2016.

I knew in my heart that I had to quit drinking. I knew it was time. I was reckless, my health was deteriorating, I was gaining weight, and I wasn't feeling good, but I did have her in my life, which really gave me a good, solid foundation of something other than myself—because I couldn't depend on myself at the time.

At the end of 2016, I decided to quit drinking. Initially, I just wanted to quit for a month or two, but after I got through a couple of months, I decided I wanted to do a full year. People often ask me, "What was the point when you hit rock bottom and knew you needed to change?"

Really, I just drew a line in the sand. I had my last drink on December 28, 2016, for at least the next twelve months. Little did I know at the time that, six months from then, I was going to get the most shocking news of my life and would have to relive the pain of death once again.

SAYING GOODBYE... AGAIN

By the time July 2017 rolled around, I had been sober for six months. I look back and realize this was such a blessing.

I had been doing a lot of personal development work that year—a lot of manifesting work, a lot of gratitude. I was allowing myself to feel the shit that I needed to feel in order to heal. A lot of people ask me about my routine. It was gratitude journaling, exercise, and meditation. Those three things were so important to me; with them, I was able to build on the foundation versus having to dig myself out of holes every single day.

I had started working for another hotel company as a bar manager and was in a completely different headspace. I was able to work in an environment where I had control of my life, instead of taking my power away and making stupid mistakes. I was feeling good, and I was feeling empowered. I thank the Universe and God so much to this day that I was in that head space when I got the terrible news.

I was sitting at home one morning when my brother contacted me, saying, "Dad has forty-eight hours to live. He has Stage 4 cancer. They just found it, and you need to get back to Canada right now and see him."

Once again, I was in denial. *There's no way that's possible. This only happens in movies. It doesn't happen to me.*

And there it was again—that sick-to-my-stomach feeling. I was so upset, I cried. I was just so low and broken, thinking about losing my dad just after we'd started to come back together again. When I think back now, I am so grateful I wasn't in the spiral of drinking and doing drugs at the time. I'm so grateful I had a strong foundation to get me through that moment, because it was so challenging emotionally. I had so much stuff that needed to be taken care of that I wouldn't have been able to do, if I'd been in that state. I now believe I had an intuitive knowledge that I needed to prepare my body for this tragedy.

After receiving this devastating news, I headed for the airport. My dad called while I was checking in. He told me I'd better get out there, because it wasn't looking good. Hearing those words from my dad just broke my heart.

I got on a plane back to Canada, and almost twenty hours later, I finally arrived at the hospital at around noon. It was my first flight ever without alcohol since I was twenty-one. At that point, my dad was still very coherent. He knew I was there, but I could tell he was in enormous pain. He was on medication, and slowly, throughout the day, they started to give him more and more.

Watching him go into this state is something I'll never forget; it's burned into my brain for the rest of my life. I watched them feed him these drugs, these painkillers I don't even know he wanted, and serve him food I wouldn't serve to my worst enemy. (The stuff they feed people in hospitals is an absolute disgrace. Why they serve that stuff to people on their deathbeds while they're in the hospital, instead of serving them nutrient-dense food, is beyond me. It's really just a disgusting thing.)

As we sat there, I watched him deteriorate for the next few hours. A couple of other people came in and said their goodbyes. We just looked after him, knowing that the end was near.

Because I was still in the same clothes from flying sixteen hours straight, I thought I had a little bit of time, so I went home to my dad's house and had a shower. I had this weird thought that maybe, if I made him a green smoothie, it would bring him back to life.

When I was at my dad's house, I got a call informing me that my dad had passed away. I went back to the hospital and said my final goodbye.

To this day, I still look back and don't understand what happened. My dad's doctors—a naturopath, a functional medicine doctor, and a general practitioner—didn't see this coming. The fact that he was told to stop being a hypochondriac and not worry so much when he felt something wasn't right just a few weeks prior is heartbreaking. The medical system really let us down in this situation, and it's sad because we lost a great man who really did his best to look after himself.

One thing I really learned about the situation is the negative physical impact that emotional stress and trauma, like losing a loved one, can have on a person's health. Prior to this, over a six-year period, I had lost my grandpa, my grandma, and two great uncles, all of whom we were very close with. My dad also lost one of his best friends growing up and a couple of other close family friends, in addition to his son. Since 2010, there were six or seven people lost. I don't think his body could handle the heartbreak.

This is part of the reason why I do what I do today. This experience helped me realize the importance of handling our emotions during stressful situations that we have no control over. Adversity is coming, no matter what. We have a choice, however, about how we react and how we process those emotions.

Once my father died, I knew that my life had to change. I knew I had to make a difference in my life. I knew I had to get out of the bar industry and pursue something else. I didn't know what that was; I just knew the path I was on wasn't serving my higher self, my intuition, my heart, my inner knowing.

My ego thought, *Well, if I continue to work in this industry, I'll be able to pay all the bills and do things I want to do*, but in my heart, I knew it wasn't the right direction. I also knew, if I wasn't following my soul, I was doing myself a disservice.

I believe that the Universe will keep throwing things in your way when you're not on the right path, until you pay attention—and I was paying attention. I knew in my heart I was destined to do something great. I knew in my heart I needed to do something of impact.

After everything I had gone through—having to leave my family, being bullied in school, dealing with a stepmom from hell, dealing with drug and alcohol abuse, and losing family members; all of that stuff added up—I knew I was either going to be a victim to this and allow myself to deteriorate or step into empowerment, learn, and grow.

UNIVERSITY OF ADVERSITY

In 2018, I came back to Canada to create a new life and take steps forward in a new direction. I decided to start a podcast, *University of Adversity*, where I could interview people who had been through challenging times. The purpose of my podcast is to inspire people to change their perspective on adversity, so they feel empowered in whatever struggle they're facing.

At the end of the day, how we look at the adversity ahead of us is all based on our past. It's all based on the stories we have lived; we take those stories and relive them in the present moment. Since much of our perspective on challenges and struggles creates an emotional attachment, we cultivate an expectation about how something should be. When we approach adversity this way, it results in a lot of pain. But we have the opportunity to grow from every single challenge we face. We have the opportunity in the invitation to step into this and dance with it and work with it, because, on the other side of it, we know there's that treasure we seek, that growth we desire. We all want to be the best we can be.

After interviewing 350 of the most inspirational and successful people on the planet—*New York Times* bestselling authors, professional athletes, celebrities, serial entrepreneurs, doctors, scientists, spiritual masters, and the common heroes among us—I've been able to understand that people look at the challenges ahead of them differently. Some people look at it as a game; some people purposely put themselves through shit all the time so that, when things come, it's not a big deal.

It really is how you look at it. You have the opportunity to look at this thing from a different perspective. That's the whole point of this book—to share the stories that will help you shift your perspective of your pain into purpose and use it to your advantage.

We all have these stories, and we all have a past. If we don't work on trying to process the trauma and all of the emotions that come with it, we are going to relive our present pain into the future.

Awareness is the first step. That's why it's so important to hear other people's stories and connect with someone who has been through something similar. It can change your perspective. That's where the inner work begins.

This book will take you on a journey to show you how it's possible to make adversity your advantage. I hope to be a living example of this for you. The road never gets any easier, but how we experience it and look at it does.

CHAPTER 2

DEFINING ADVERSITY

"When we least expect it, life sets up a challenge to test our courage and willingness to change; at such a moment, there is no point in pretending that nothing has happened or in saying that we are not yet ready. The challenge will not wait. Life does not look back."
—Paulo Coelho

Whatever you want to call your challenges, whether they are obstacles, difficulties, resistance, or struggle, adversity generally is some sort of block in the road in front of you. There are different types of adversity, and most of us will experience all types of adversity at some point.

Adversity can present itself romantically, socially, physically, spiritually, financially, and professionally. These adverse life events will show up in all different shapes and forms. And they will usually show up when we least expect them or aren't ready for them. Adversity will always test you and force you to dig deep. That is why I want you to be ready for every kind of adversity, at all times. Even more, when adversity does strike, I want you to get to a point where you can welcome it because you know that life's gifts are on the other side of overcoming the experience. It's not the adversity itself that will be the most challenging part; it's your perspective on it and how you react. I want to help you change your entire perspective on adversity.

Adversity will range on a spectrum from very small to very challenging, but it is important to note that the degree to which we look at things as challenging is really a reflection of how we look at life in general. If we are living in lack, we will always see the negative in hardship. On the contrary, if we are seeing the lesson and the gift in the Universe rerouting our path, we will always see the opportunity. Sometimes, the adversity that's in front of you may look a lot more challenging on a certain day. Then, the same type of experience happens on another day, and it's much easier to deal with. So, my conclusion is that adversity is all about perspective.

When I was younger, I used to look at adversity in my life and the challenges I faced as being these things that got in the way of the success I deserved. I felt entitled to ease and accomplishment, yet I wasn't really being real with myself when it came to the amount of work and self-belief that was needed to actually achieve all of the things I felt entitled to. So, when these roadblocks came and they challenged me, I didn't have the mindset to understand that this thing in front of me that I was looking at was going to allow me to grow, learn, and eventually get past it.

As we start to grow as human beings, the inherent challenges in the adversity we face will not be the same as they were when we encountered similar situations previously, because our perspectives have changed.

I used to look at adversity from a "Why me?" point of view. I always felt like a victim of circumstance. I assumed everything was supposed to go smoothly or else I was a failure. What I didn't understand was that the adversity I was experiencing was actually the medicine I needed in my life to get better as a person. If everything were easy, we wouldn't appreciate it, we wouldn't grow, and we wouldn't get better. Over the years, I learned that adversity is essential in teaching us the lessons we need to get to the level we want. Most people see adversity as bad, but if we really understand that, on the other side of adversity, there is bliss, growth, enjoyment, and a sense of accomplishment, we learn to seek it.

Over the years, after healing from my own traumas and stories of the past and through listening to the stories of those whom I've interviewed, I have been able to look at adversity as a vital part of my success. If we don't go through adversity, we don't get fulfillment, because we're living on autopilot. There are other ways to create fulfillment in your life, but there is something pretty special about the feeling of overcoming a real challenge. We all want that feeling of peace, and we all enjoy it when things are smooth sailing, but all of us have an inner yearning to grow, and in order to grow, we have to go through some shit.

Over the years, I've realized that, in order for me to have ever been able to do what I'm doing—writing this book, building a company, hosting a successful podcast, creating courses, and making a difference in my own life—I had to overcome a certain amount of adversity. Now, I look at it as absolutely essential. And I know that more is coming for me no matter what. So I want to provide to you the tools I've learned, because in order for you to be able to get through adversity, you're going to have to shift your perspective from victimhood to ownership. This is often easier said than done, but the journey of life is really about understanding that adversity is unavoidable. We might as well put on the body armor so that, when it does come, we're ready for it.

The beautiful thing about hearing others' stories of overcoming adversity is that it not only empowers us, but it inspires us, and it helps us build resilience. When you heal your trauma and push through adversity, you're not only empowering yourself, but you're inspiring others around you. What I have noticed is that being able to see that we are all human, that we all have stories of the past, that we all have adversity in our lives, is how we can build resilience. The people who are winning in life—the people who are the happiest and most successful, whether that be with money, friends, family, or opportunities—are the ones who become empowered. They get inspired by others, and they build up resilience and belief in themselves.

The hard things we don't want to look at—the things that scare us, the things that cause that response of fear and anxiety—are the things we need to lean into the most, because our body is giving us a sign. It's testing us. When we overcome something challenging, it rarely presents itself in reality in the same way as it did in our minds. It's often not nearly as bad as we think it's going to be, yet we still go back to the same programming of wanting to stop and worry about the adversity in front of us. We're still in the fear of the struggle.

Moving through this is a constant process that takes time. Some of us learn this lesson more quickly than others because we are more practiced. Seeking challenge in everyday life and putting ourselves in uncomfortable positions conditions us, so when something real actually happens, it's not a big deal. When we face our fears and challenges, it is an indicator of our strength.

If facing adversity is difficult, we need to become conscious of what is holding us back and why we keep telling ourselves the same stories; that is the real challenge—going back and healing the shit that is holding us back. Nobody is broken; there are things we are going to go through in life that will get in the way sometimes. If you aren't conditioned to fail over and over and over again, or if you think it's a bad thing when you do, then you're never going to move forward.

Adversity is the biggest component of revealing your character. Everybody can be great when things are easy, but how are you when things are tough and when you're going through the shitstorm? This is the transition in my life that I am currently working on. I am empowering myself with the tools, the tips, and the resources to create a better mindset, a better perspective, of the obstacles in front of me, because doing so makes life easier.

I know the challenges aren't going to go away because they're essential to my growth. And I know that because of learning from so many people. This is why I'm writing his book—so you can read this from start to finish and come away with a completely different perspective on the adversity you face in your life. When you do, you can build more resilience, feel empowered, and live out that inspired feeling that you have inside of you. If you're clear on where you want to go and you come from a place of truth and inspiration, then you're going to understand that all of this shit we go through is essential. When you become powerful, resilient, and inspirational, you're going to allow others in the world to do the same.

FOCUS ON YOURSELF

The problem in the world that we face right now is that everybody is pointing the finger at each other and not at themselves. Everybody is focused on what should be done and the things that are going wrong. If all of us were to focus all of that energy inward, on what we're doing individually every day and how we think and on healing ourselves and our stories so we can be empowered, then massive change would occur on this planet.

When we empower ourselves, when we heal the shit that is holding us back and take action to control our own lives, that gives other people around us the permission to do the same. From there, it's a ripple effect. When you are at your highest and doing your best and you are not pointing fingers, then you shine your brightest light and emit your highest vibration. Then, the people around you cannot help but feed off that energy. Imagine if, today, everybody took it upon themselves to really get clear on what was going on with their stories, to change their perspectives so they didn't look at life from the victim's perspective anymore, and to accept their circumstances and appreciate life in the moment.

GRATITUDE IN DARKNESS

Showing gratitude in the adversity, gratitude in the struggle, is how we will actually learn the lesson we are being taught. Showing gratitude is easy when things are going well, but ask yourself: What kind of gratitude do you show when your back is up against the wall? When shit is hitting the fan? How much gratitude do you have for the moment? How much can you say to the Universe, to God, that you are grateful for what you're going through, because you are going to learn and because you're going to grow? That's the key. That's what shows our true character—how we show up in the face of adversity.

It's not easy. It's very hard for people, including myself, to show gratitude when things are hard. We immediately go into victim programming, especially considering what's going on in the world right now. We want to blame others, and we want to look outside ourselves for answers. Instead, let's just look at ourselves. Are we showing up? Are we doing our best? What are we taking in? This is where the change happens. We have to start with ourselves. Empowered individuals create an empowered society. This is not an easy solution, but knowing this is a start.

This is why it's important to be super clear on your own story, on your own journey, and how you show up in the world. Understanding why I do certain things has changed my life and my perspective on adversity.

In a challenging moment, I will now ask myself, *Why am I thinking about this in this way? Am I telling a story that's true? Or am I holding onto a past belief that isn't true? Why am I so afraid of this challenge? Why does this adversity make me so uncomfortable, when I know what I can do? When I know I can overcome it, and I know, on the other side of it, I'm going to feel more empowered, more resilient?*

Then, I make a conscious decision: *I'm going to have more courage.* It's challenging—this is the journey of life—but you have to continue to commit to bringing out the best of yourself.

CHAPTER 3

THE FOUR ADVERSITY ARCHETYPES

"When we are no longer able to change a situation, we are challenged to change ourselves."
— Viktor Frankl

When faced with adversity, we tend to approach it in a few different ways. How you face the adversity in front of you has a lot to do with your past and how you dealt with adversity prior to this moment. Your actions in these challenging moments are influenced by the stories you tell yourself about the past.

Our past stories, if we aren't conditioning our mind to create new ones, will usually run the programs in our lives in the present moment. So, if you're used to doing certain things when challenges come, then chances are you will continue to do those, unless you do the work and make the changes within—healing your trauma and your limiting beliefs, and changing the story you tell yourself about how you see adversity.

I've broken down the ways a human shows up in the face of adversity into four different archetypes—the Distractor, the Victim, the Fixer, and the Warrior. These archetypes are distinct and recognizable, but there are some common traits that overlap within them, too. We have all shown up as each of these archetypes at some point or another. Once you have knowledge of them, you will be able to identify which one of these archetypes you are showing up as in a given situation, with the eventual goal of moving toward the warrior archetype.

The point isn't judgment; it's for you to be aware of your patterns of behavior. That way, when these patterns arise, you can step into awareness of how past wounds are affecting your choices, and you can make a conscious effort to create new responses instead of falling into a familiar past and running the old programs in the present moment.

THE 4 ADVERSITY ARCHETYPES DEFINED

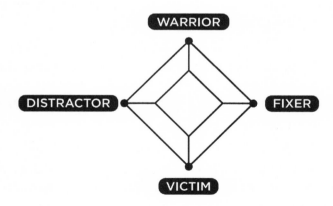

ADVERSITY ARCHETYPE #1: DISTRACTOR

The Distractor chooses the path of numbing and escaping to avoid feeling uncomfortable emotions. This is the archetype that will experience the highest level of secondary emotions—emotions like anger, anxiety, depression, and exhaustion—because they are continuously sweeping their true feelings under the rug and never processing them. This often spirals into addiction, which can include anything from drugs and alcohol to food, sex, porn, television, and overworking.

Getting stuck in the busy trap is one of the characteristics of the Distractor. The Distractor can achieve a high level of success, as they have learned to take their escapism and channel it into staying busy and productive, but this is still a trauma response and a survival tactic based on a story.

In our world, we can be rewarded for this behavior, so we feel there is nothing wrong with it. There is a certain amount of drive we need to be successful, which our ego feeds into. What's important here is cultivating awareness by asking yourself:

> ➢ "Why do I feel I need to continue being so busy?"
>
> ➢ "Who is this for, and who taught me this is the way?"
>
> ➢ "Why do I feel the need to numb myself and run from my emotions?"
>
> ➢ "Where in my life am I feeling deep shame?"
>
> ➢ "What am I trying to avoid or ignore by always needing to focus on something outside myself?"

The Distractor tends to use work or other vices when they feel a stress response or when they feel as though they're facing challenges. They experience nervousness and anxiety and will reach for something that's going to distract them from the present moment. That temporary relief becomes something they crave, and this craving can turn into a full-blown addiction. While it can feel like escape, a toxic cycle it is actually being created. The Distractor uses these vices in an attempt to avoid an emotional experience linked to their past trauma. But when you distract, you aren't developing healthy coping skills for when the going gets tough.

People don't want to become addicts; they're seeking a feeling of wholeness, and addictive substances allow them to escape discomfort for a moment. If these escapist tendencies are repeated over time, they can very easily become a habit without the person realizing it, until it has become a problem.

What do you do when you're under stress? Do you reach for alcohol or drugs? Do you eat? Do you feel the need for sex or porn? Do you feel the need to look on your phone and see what everybody else is doing? Do you feel the need to always be busy? Do you clean the house to distract yourself? Do you go shopping? Do you feel that being at home and being present isn't enough, so you have to go do other things?

If you are in this habit of distracting yourself whenever you face adversity or a challenge, you need to be aware of it, because the longer this goes on, the worse the situation will feel. The feeling of avoiding something you know you need to deal with head-on can start to weigh on you after a while.

This behavior of distracting and diverting from challenge or discomfort in the present moment is something almost all humans do in some way or another, and this need to escape happens more often when we feel depressed or lonely. This doesn't just have to be with adversity or a big hardship you need to face; this Distractor archetype can also show up in small tasks or minor discomforts we avoid. This resistance is normal and is typically termed *avoidance* or *procrastination*.

Each person has their own unique way of being a Distractor, and some have no idea that they are even doing it. The more awareness of these behaviors you have, the more you'll be able to identify them and consciously choose a behavior you actually want, rather than unconsciously reacting on autopilot. So, what do you do when small challenges arise? Do you distract yourself? Or do you fully embrace the discomfort?

This is really important to be aware of because our whole society—the media and information age—is designed to encourage these Distractor behaviors. It can look like something as simple as ordering and consuming too much food to take our mind off what we have to face. The corporations that drive consumerism notice what eases our minds and will provide us with things that will "save" us when we are not feeling at ease.

An important component when it comes to dissecting the Distractor archetype is physical adversity or adversity due to poor health. Physical adversity can arise when we lean on vices such as the ones mentioned above—food, alcohol, drugs, sex, partying, etc. By now, I believe we all have an understanding of the link between physical and mental/emotional health. Disregarding one's physical health is dangerous, because when this is in jeopardy, it inhibits our ability to think clearly. This is not just because of the obvious impairment that occurs with certain substances, but also the longer-term effects of lack of energy and, in some cases, deterioration of our vital organs. The state of our physical health can make or break us when we are moving through adversity. It can completely change our perspective on a situation.

When you're physically doing the right things, it's like you're putting on body armor for whatever comes your way. When you move your body, you're sweating, you're creating endorphins, and you're releasing toxins. All of this leads to making healthier food choices and drinking more water. In this state, you'll be more likely to have awareness of what you might be lacking nutritionally and gravitate toward what will benefit your body and brain.

In this peak state of health, you have more energy, and you tend to deal with challenging situations with much more ease. Your perspective on what is occurring changes for the better. Things roll off your back easier. When your body feels good, so does your mind. You have a better mental capacity to deal with whatever the Universe decides to throw at you.

ADVERSITY ARCHETYPE #2: VICTIM

This archetype is one of the most challenging ones to get out of. A lot of Victim mentality comes from a troubled past. Generally, the person who experiences a Victim mentality is somebody who focuses on what could go wrong versus what will go right. The glass is always half empty versus half full. The person with the Victim mentality is generally in survival mode, not in creative, thrive, or solution mode.

It's important to identify this because, if we remain unaware, it becomes challenging to change our thoughts and habits that perpetuate the pattern of victimhood. Once we become aware of the way we think about the adversity we are experiencing, we can choose more empowering thoughts.

This is not an easy process, because a lot of how we view our life and the world is rooted in trauma. There's a certain amount of healing that needs to happen in order to break free from the emotional attachment of the past, your emotions that connect you to certain things.

Some of the characteristics in this archetype are wallowing in your own sadness, blaming others, being a prisoner in your own mind, constantly talking about how bad everything is, a doom-and-gloom outlook, feeling stuck all the time, feeling like the world is coming to an end, feeling lack instead of feeling gratitude, feeling like everything around you is a problem, and feeling as though problems are everyone else's fault. When you are in a victim mentality, there is no accountability for yourself, and you're looking for other people to fix your problems.

Unfortunately, right now, most people fall into this category. People in our society are looking for others to be responsible for their health and happiness, and instead of taking ownership of their own lives, they are expending the same amount of energy pointing the finger and expecting others to have the answers or to rescue them. These people are living with constant feelings of entitlement; they blame others for not having control over their own lives. It is the out-of-balance energy, the woundedness that we wear on our sleeves so all can see, in order to achieve validation for our pain.

I want to make it very clear that we cannot always control what happens in our lives. A lot of very challenging moments have happened to a lot of people, which has created massive emotional stress and trauma in their lives. If you're one of these people, I'm not here to judge, shame, or discredit you. But I am here to say, now that that experience has passed, it is up to you to be conscious about how you go about subsequent challenges. You can't choose what happens to you, but you can choose how you react. That's what it's going to take to step into a more empowered role in your own life.

ADVERSITY ARCHETYPE #3: FIXER

The Fixer is on the path to becoming the Warrior, the final archetype, and to being empowered, but is still overcompensating in certain areas and still isn't taking ownership over his/her life. The Fixer hasn't really gotten to the root of what is causing them to behave the way they do.

They are somebody who feels a sense of brokenness. They blame themselves all the time; they're very hard on themselves and always looking for solutions outside of themselves to fix who they are. In other words, they're very dependent on others to always know "better." The Fixer gets caught in the trap of what others are selling instead of trusting themselves. There is often a false expectation attached to an outcome they believe the outside source will bring.

This archetype is characterized by a lack of self-trust and a lack of self-confidence. This person overloads on personal development, but they don't apply what they've been taught, or if they do, it's only for a very short time, because they don't truly believe in themselves. They attend personal development events and conferences but fail to integrate the lessons in their day-to-day life. This is somebody who constantly reads books but doesn't apply the knowledge.

Fixers are people-pleasers and have no real sense of who they truly are. The act of pleasing others just pushes them further away from themselves. This archetype is definitely a step up from the Victim as far as making the path forward to attempted healing and growing, but it's still stuck in a level of woundedness.

The Fixer consciously believes they are helping themselves, but on a subconscious level, they are essentially looking for things outside themselves to save them.

This archetype has a level of self-awareness, but they're still not completely owning and building that confidence within themselves. They haven't really dialed in the confidence they need in order to trust themselves, and they aren't really going in and looking at themselves or the things they can fully control every single day that will help build their confidence.

Sometimes, people are okay with the answers they're given. You see this in the personal-development world. A Fixer can feel like a forever-broken person. They're waiting for permission to do what they already know. They feel they always need different answers and are never satisfied. They go from one place to another and never really apply what they've learned.

I've noticed this is predominant in the spiritual space—in the plant-medicine realm. I've witnessed a lot of people who have gotten into the trap of trying to chase the next experience—the next psychedelic medicine—without integrating the lessons they've learned on that particular journey. These people were given homework and takeaways from these plant medicines—insights into their lives and their higher selves.

Some people are so addicted to being healed and so addicted to their story, they are resigned to feel "broken" forever. Because of this, the answer they got from this particular experience isn't enough; it isn't the right one. They continue to chase the next one to see if they like it better or if they can get something novel out of that experience.

If this sounds like you, just be mindful as to why you are continuing to chase new experiences. Have you fully integrated the ones you have already experienced? Have you given yourself enough time to digest and make meaning of those experiences? The Fixer, in this day and age, has to work against so much with the amount of information that's constantly coming at us to do more, be better, and consume, consume, consume.

Imagine speed-reading twenty books in a week and how challenging it would be to integrate that information, because each book is its own journey in itself. If you don't decide which book you're going to apply, you're going to start getting conflicting information. Then, you're going to start to question what is true. So, what happens is you consume too much information too frequently, and then you don't know how to decipher what's true and what's not.

This is important to remember if you decide to explore plant medicine or psychedelics. You get such deep insights and you are connecting to such powerful energy. It's a beautiful space. You must honor the medicine and give it the time it needs to integrate.

Whatever journey you're on, just honor yourself—whether you are called to do more medicine or read more books. Also, remember that there are seasons. There are seasons to plant seeds, seasons to harvest, and there are seasons to reap the benefits of all this personal development—to start to apply what you've learned.

I remember hearing Jim Rohn talk about this concept of seasons, and it really stuck with me. I was in this loop of consuming personal-development material but not producing change, thinking that was what I needed, because I literally felt like I had to reprogram and learn things I'd never learned before. Now I'm at the point, and writing this book is an example of this, where I'm in creation mode. I am not consuming as much; instead, I'm getting content out there, creating courses, and building community, because this is my time to harvest. When it's time for me to reap the benefits of that harvest, then I'll probably take the foot off the gas and enjoy that for a bit, before I get going again. Life is full of these cycles, and it's important to be aware of them.

That process of being aware of where you are in this cycle is really important. Understand that, if you are embodying the Fixer archetype. Also, if you relate to this archetype and you're constantly focused on the fact that you're lacking or need to be someone else, just know that you are whole and perfect as you are. It is through releasing layers of conditioning that you will find your answers within yourself.

I am the first to admit that it is a challenge to sit and unpack the feelings and emotions we all have. Most people don't give themselves the space to be still and process what they're feeling. There's always something to divert them from what actually matters, for whatever reason.

If you are somebody who is trying to fix yourself with external resources, I encourage you to ask yourself why that is. Start to slow down and journal about some of the things you've learned but haven't applied yet. Journal about why you have been chasing the next thing. Ask yourself why that answer is more important than the ones you already have. You'll be surprised at what you find.

ADVERSITY ARCHETYPE #4: WARRIOR

I call this archetype the Warrior because I feel this word best represents what it means to personify all of the traits that we need in order to face and overcome adversity or challenge.

As I mentioned in the Introduction, society has a flawed perception of what it means to be a warrior. The word invokes images of someone who wants to fight; someone who wants to go to war. Although the word "war" is in the word "warrior," that's not necessarily what it means.

The Warrior possesses a lot of very powerful qualities that I believe are the reason we are all here today. Our ancestors had to have this warrior energy within them in order to get through some of the most challenging situations ever imagined—battle, famine, economic depression. Your ancestors must have had a certain amount of Warrior energy to make it through these challenging times and to give you the life you now have. If your family were refugees and came from a different country, they had to have a certain amount of Warrior energy to have faith and trust that they were going somewhere that would work out for them.

The Warrior possesses all the energy of empowerment; they are empowered human beings who take complete ownership of their lives. They have open hearts, they are patient, they face their fears, they are self-aware, and they are aware of the people and the circumstances around them. They take a step back to look at what is going on when a challenge arises. They take the time to learn all of the facts and then make the best decision. They are patient, they are compassionate to the people around them, and they are compassionate with themselves.

They are on a mission to create unity and connection within the people around them, not division. They stand in their truth, and they are able to tell what is right versus what is wrong and live in this integrity. In order to be able to do that, Warriors tap into their intuition; into their higher selves. They are able to essentially sit in the driver's seat of their life versus being the passenger. They show grace for the people around them, including their enemies. They are solution-focused, and they are grounded and centered in the face of a challenge.

Most importantly, the Warrior possesses immense gratitude. They understand gratitude is the ultimate state to receive all of their desires. Warriors are able to look at adversity as essential for growth. They see the full picture when moving through challenges, and they are quick to see the lessons and the gift within the experience, detaching from "good" and "bad," and instead accepting what is. They have cultivated a healthy level of stoicism and flow through the unexpected.

This is obviously the most powerful and most healed archetype, and it is the one we all strive to embody. Sometimes, slowing down, getting a deeper understanding, and learning how to listen is more important than expressing your opinions and your emotions to the world. Being able to channel the inner wisdom in that inner energy into yourself, into your healing, is really what's going to make change happen. Someone who can do this is a true leader.

The Warrior is able to encourage the people around them to shine by being able to see them for who they are and their special gifts versus what they lack. To be able to identify somebody's gifts, even if they may not see them themselves, and to help empower them to apply those gifts is one of the greatest qualities a leader can have—being someone who can see the greatness within others and helping them bring it to light.

If we are mindful of the Warrior, the Distractor, the Fixer, and the Victim within all of us and if we know which characteristics we possess, we can start to better understand where we need to make changes to benefit our future. Nobody is perfect, and we're not supposed to be perfect. That's the beauty of life—identifying where we can improve and doing our best in the moment.

The Warrior is simply the observer of the wounded archetypes, leading us back to love and healing whenever we may stray off course. Therefore, it's important to look at these archetypes and really understand them and where they are showing up. With awareness, you can identify them and then start to make new choices on how you react.

I want you to really look at these archetypes and ask yourself, "Which one do I show up as most frequently?"

This isn't a shame exercise; this is just an awareness exercise. We cannot heal what we do not allow ourselves to see and feel. We cannot change our perspectives on life and adversity unless we are aware of our behaviors. Once we are aware, then we can have accountability; then we can take ownership. And then, we can be aware of the habits that pop up based on our thoughts. Once we can be mindful of them, we can adopt new ones.

Archetype	Embodiment
DISTRACTOR	• Emotionally unavailable • Disconnected from self • Numbing as a coping mechanism • Avoids conflict • Difficulty communicating emotions • Selfishness • All or nothing mentality • Compartmentalizes feelings • Attaches to vices/Addictions: alcohol, drugs, food, sex, porn, TV, overworking, busyness, shopping, etc.
VICTIM	• Shame/insecurity • Wallows and blames others • Prisoner complex/feel stuck • Engages in trauma bonding • In lack vs. gratitude • "Everything is a problem" mentality • Manipulative/has tantrums • Wants to be saved • Drowning in emotions

FIXER	• Brokenness/blames themselves
	• Controlling/Lack of self-trust
	• People-pleaser/Always says "Yes"
	• Seeks outside solutions
	• Afraid of failure
	• Overloads on personal development
	• Extremely self-critical
	• Frequent negative self-talk
	• Thrives off external validation
WARRIOR	• Heart-centered decisions
	• Empowered
	• Takes ownership
	• Opportunity vs. lack mentality
	• Resilience and grace
	• Strong intuition/Connected to self
	• Stands in core values
	• Practices self-love & self-care
	• Solution-oriented
	• Cultivates gratitude
	• Observer (vs. Judge) of the shadow-self
	• Unattached
	• Looks within for answers

ENERGETIC UNDERPINNINGS

Another way to look at the four adversity archetypes is in terms of the energetic imbalances that characterize the wounded archetypes (Distractor, Victim, Fixer) and the energetic balance that is characteristic of the Warrior. When referring to energy in this section, we will be focused exclusively on masculine and feminine energy.

When many people hear the words "feminine" or "masculine," they automatically associate this with gender. However, for this section, I invite you to look past that, so you can have a better understanding of the concept.

Every human being has both masculine and feminine energy, and being able to access both masculine and feminine energy is *very* important. Most people are out of balance, however, and are dominant in one area—men, especially, are skewed imbalanced in favor of masculine energy. Ideally, we want to shoot for equilibrium.

The reasons for being dominant in one versus another can come from a person's upbringing, values, beliefs, trauma, relationships, social media—the list goes on. It's important to recognize where you're out of balance, so you can begin to adjust your behaviors to bring these energies to equilibrium.

So, what are masculine and feminine energy, exactly?

Masculine energy refers to the energy of *doing*, which is usually fueled by logic and reason. Masculine energy is very powerful and can help create a lot of success in your life, but it can also easily become out of balance. Examples of qualities and actions associated with masculine energy include strength, leadership, courage, discipline, hustling, risk-taking, competition, standing up for your beliefs, logic, self-assurance, and structure.

Sometimes people will overexaggerate these characteristics in order to compensate for a lack in their life or an unhealed wound from the past. When used properly and in balance with feminine energy, however, this masculine energy can take you to amazing places.

Setting goals, having a daily discipline like a morning routine, creating a plan or structure in your life, and standing up and speaking your mind are all examples of masculine activities that can help you to overcome adversity.

Feminine energy is a state of *being*. It is more of an intuitive feeling, the ability to allow the flow of life to occur and exist in the state of receiving. Examples of qualities and actions associated with feminine energy include heart-centeredness, gratitude, compassion, empathy, creativity, intuition, acceptance, love, self-reflection, wisdom, understanding, and patience.

Yoga, meditation, and journaling are a couple of examples of feminine-energy activities that I have utilized in my own life to develop a deeper understanding of myself; this has led me to become better at the masculine tasks, which seemed to require so much more pushing and effort before.

The more tapped into the feminine energy you are, you will actually become more productive and more efficient at the masculine activities. You will be become a more well-rounded human with a deeper sense of peace and will develop a more holistic perspective.

Somewhere along the way, our society lost understanding of the importance of feminine energy, and it has been greatly misunderstood ever since. The good news is, once it is better understood and harnessed with the masculine energy, you are literally unstoppable.

CHAPTER 4

TRAUMA

"The wound is where the Light enters you."
— Rumi

Much of our maladaptive coping mechanisms (Distractor behaviors and Victim mentality) originate with some form of trauma. The first step in overcoming trauma is getting a clear picture of the situation.

So, how do we define trauma? And how do we know if we have experienced trauma?

According to Dr. Gabor Maté, psychologist, author, and expert in trauma, stress, addiction, and childhood development, "Trauma is a psychic wound that hardens you psychologically and then interferes with your ability to grow and develop. It pains you, and now you're acting out of pain. It induces fear, and now you're acting out of fear. Trauma is not what happens to you. It's what happens inside you as a result of what happened to you. Trauma is that scarring that makes you less flexible, more rigid, less feeling, and more defended."

The best way to notice whether or not you have a trauma response is by paying attention to whether or not you have emotional triggers. Do you feel emotions of heightened intensity following certain situations that wouldn't evoke the same intensity in others? Recognize the emotion that surfaces, how often you feel that emotion when it happens, and your behavior following that emotion.

For example, when I was about four years old, I was thrown into the deep end of a pool by a swimming instructor, and I felt like I was drowning. After that, I wouldn't go near water until I was eleven. My mom couldn't even get me in the bathtub. I was so horrified.

I had partially worked through this, but even to this day, I feel a slight level of fear of going into unknown waters on a boat ride or surfing.

RECOGNIZING SUBCONSCIOUS PROGRAMMING

If you really think about it, every single negative response you have—such as anger, resentment, shame, and fear—was learned somewhere, at some point. If you have a trauma response, when something triggers you or reminds you of the event that once happened, you will experience similar emotions to when the traumatic event happened originally.

Most people don't even realize that this subconscious programming is running, because this stuff starts at such a young age. Everything we are today—our beliefs, our identity, how we look at the world, the emotions we feel—was learned mostly between birth and age ten. Children at that age don't have a filter or a way to distinguish whether something is good or bad, because we have nothing else to compare it to. So, we end up absorbing everything that comes in.

If you are surrounded by negativity and anger, you will store that in your subconscious. At that age, you don't have a way of distinguishing what is good versus what isn't, so if you are constantly surrounded by people's negative emotions and anger, then that's generally who you will become later. If you are surrounded by love and positive energy, then you will be able to absorb that and become more of that in your life later on.

LOOKING BACK WITH OBJECTIVITY AND GRATITUDE

When I look back at my own story of trauma, it started at a very young age. For many years after my parents split up, I played the victim role. I was upset at my mom for leaving my dad and at my dad for not being a nicer person to my mom.

During my childhood, there was a ton of fighting, and money and finances were always at the root of it, so things would get very emotionally difficult. I remember feeling that emotional drama and fighting as a kid; it became what I expected and part of who I was, later on. Luckily, I also had a ton of love from my family. My parents gave me more than I could ever imagine when it comes to love. Even though they fought with each other, they provided and did the very best they could, giving us a life that most kids in our situation probably wouldn't have lived.

When I look back on when things really unraveled for me, it was when I moved across the country at age eleven. From that point through my late teens and early adulthood, things became really challenging for me, and I was traumatized by it. Now, when I look back, I'm able to find the moment when things got squirrelly in my life. Once I could pinpoint that moment, I could start to figure out how to heal it.

This is why self-awareness is so important. If you don't have self-awareness, you are never going to be able to understand where your behaviors and emotions come from. This is unique for everybody, because we've all experienced different things in different parts of our lives.

It's so important to be aware, to look at your life from a high-level perspective, and to go back into the moments that may have been challenging in order to process them, because you never had the ability to do this at the time. In most cases, when you went through a traumatizing moment, you had to do it on your own. That's very challenging for a young person, because you have this emotion but you're not yet equipped with the tools to fully process what is happening, so it gets trapped.

As life goes on, we continue looking for ways to cope to relieve that discomfort and allow ourselves to escape, even just for a moment.

UNHEALTHY COPING—DISTRACTOR BEHAVIORS IN RESPONSE TO TRAUMA

Most people who experience deep trauma are just looking to feel better; whether they end up getting addicted to something or they try to change their life, they just want to feel better.

When we are suffering, all we want is to find a way to end that suffering through any means necessary. So, when you discover something like drugs, alcohol, sex, or whatever it may be, if it gives you that feeling of completeness and wholeness in the moment, you seek out that feeling of comfort, even if it's only temporary. You chase that first high—sometimes literally, sometimes figuratively.

Addictive behaviors happen to all of us and do not discriminate. They are a means of control and attachment to a story of what we think we need. Addictions don't necessarily need to be alcohol or illegal substances. We can get addicted to things like sugar; we can get addicted to things that produce dopamine hits, such as our cell phones and social media. It can be whatever that thing is that allows you to divert your attention from feeling the present moment.

Remember, when we do this, we are embodying the Distractor. This isn't a judgment; as humans, we have adapted to functioning this way. Most people aren't comfortable with feeling the true, deep, dark, raw emotions that are tied to our trauma. These feelings are generally buried, so there is a lack of awareness of emotions tied to memories and events that go way back. That discomfort causes us to want to run away and escape from it.

If we are able to identify what it is we're running from or acknowledge that we're even running at all, then we can gain an understanding about how that emotion and our behavior come from a story we gave meaning to. What happens next? We are able to start the work toward changing that story.

Most all of us link our trauma to our identity. But our trauma is *not* us; it is what happened to us. And an even more powerful statement to begin shifting your perspective on these traumatic events is that these traumatic events happened *for* us. They are not for naught. They are to show us something and help us grow toward our highest self.

If you think about it, our entire world is based on and sold the idea that we need something outside of ourselves to feel whole; to feel complete. These big companies have been selling us stuff and telling us we aren't enough or we won't be complete until we have this *thing*. People are constantly chasing this external validation, where this external thing is meant to rescue them or give them the feeling of wholeness. But if you don't get to the root of what that actually is you're going through, you will just keep chasing the carrot, getting further and further away from your truth and your healing.

Our societies condition us to feel that we are weak, that we need to be scared, and that in order for us to be safe and whole, we need to be rescued by an outside force. But the truth of the matter is we are resilient creatures. We are descendants of Warriors. We are here today because generations of our ancestors survived, getting through very difficult times, and now we are here.

Whatever you believe, whether you believe you chose to be here or you think it's an accident, we are here now, and the reality of it is we wouldn't be here if we didn't have resilience as a species. I encourage you to try to adopt the perspective that, no matter what you are going through, it's always going to be okay, and you will always be able to grow and heal from it. It may not be easy, and that's a simplified version, because a lot of us are going through very challenging times, but the first real step is just understanding that you can do this.

If you're reading this book, you already are aware that something needs to change. You want to master adversity and overcome past trauma and the emotions associated with it. You want to become a more empowered person and change how you view past experiences in your life so you can heal.

It is important to understand that the only way to move forward is to be empowered, to come from a place of love, and to understand that the goal of feeling whole happens through healing and feeling gratitude. Then, you no longer feel this constant lack that needs to be filled by another or the urge to consume or like you require validation from external sources, because we feel complete within ourselves.

We are all seeking different things to bring us that little bit of extra joy or happiness, but if we're being truthful with ourselves, we know those things will not heal our pain or trauma. This comes from within. You're here now, reading this book, ready to do the work on yourself. You are ready to ask yourself: Why am I constantly looking for something to fulfill me? *That* is when you know you are working through trauma. If you are seeking some outside force to heal you, then you are setting yourself up for a lifetime of disappointment.

When you are living your life in an effort to receive validation, you may very well receive the validation, but you'll never ever feel satisfied, and you most definitely won't ever feel whole, because no one outside of yourself can make you feel whole. No one but you can do this inner work. Healing, transforming, overcoming the adversity you face in your life—*this* is what will give you the fulfillment you seek. Not the external things.

THE LESSONS IN ADVERSITY

Humans are meant to go through things. We are meant to learn through pain; this is where we find meaning in the world. But we are not necessarily meant to suffer. If we can learn the lessons and be empowered from what we survive through, then we will reveal our true gift and our true purpose in life.

Sometimes that means going into the dark places and facing the shit we don't want to look at because, when we do, then we can process it and create a strong foundation to build off of. If we deny these emotions that feel uncomfortable, then it's just going to keep showing up in areas of our lives, and we will get stuck in a loop. Emotional responses to past trauma will keep surfacing.

TRAUMA RESPONSES

A trauma response is when something happens in your environment that triggers the emotion you experienced as a child whenever a traumatic event occurred. It's like a memory surfacing and creating an extremely uncomfortable feeling, depending on the severity of the trauma.

There are four trauma responses that occur: fight, flight, freeze, and fawn. The *fight* response is one where one's temper, anger, rage, and aggressive feelings and emotions will surface. The *flight* response is characterized by feelings of anxiety, panic, overthinking and overanalyzing, compulsive behavior, always being on the go, overachieving, and hyperactivity. The *freeze* response can be seen in avoidance behaviors, depression, struggles with decision-making, feeling the need to isolate or hibernate, lack of drive, lots of brain fog, and a lack of clarity and purpose. The *fawn* response can be seen in codependent behaviors, conflict avoidance, trying to fit in with everyone, getting others to make decisions, having a hard time standing up for oneself, difficulty saying no, and being a people pleaser.

If you are aware of these responses and you understand them, you can start to invite them in to feel them and process them. Once you can look at your trauma responses from this higher-level perspective, they will not have the power over you that they once did.

THE WOUNDED INNER CHILD

Carl Jung, renowned thinker, psychoanalyst, and author, coined the phrase "inner child." Essentially, we are all just grown-up children. What we value, what we believe, and most of our behaviors are shaped before age ten. Because we don't have the filter to distinguish our experiences in terms of right and wrong, good and bad, anything we are exposed to in our environment will get stored in our subconscious, and eventually, we will take on these experiences as our beliefs about who we are. We obviously grow up, get older, and eventually get exposed to people, things, and environments who will further shape us into who we become, but we are always, still, at the core, children.

It's important to be aware of this when dealing with children; they are literally sponges and are absorbing everything. We sometimes think, because children can't communicate as well, they don't understand. But the truth is they are actually able to retain more than grown adults. They just can't express it.

There is a lot of talk these days in the personal development world around the concept of the *wounded inner child*, as we are starting to see the powerful healing that happens when we choose to face and unpack childhood trauma and conditioning. Traumatic events often stunt our identity. We have trouble moving beyond our traumatic experiences.

I started to learn about the importance of the inner child as I started to do personal development work, as I started to become more aware of who I was. It was a great feeling—being able to go back and give my inner child a hug. I was able to go back and figure out the time when things got challenging for me, when my beliefs started changing, when I started to doubt myself and think differently. When I started to get to the root of this, it became easier to understand why I did the things I did, rather than beat myself up without any idea how to fix anything.

Think of the inner child as being the core of who you are and where all your beliefs started, but don't get too caught up in its defining you. Whatever happened to you when you were young isn't your fault. All the beliefs you have, good or bad, are just conditioning you received, and you didn't have any control over it.

Having an understanding of who that child is will allow you to understand what your inner child needs, depending on the wounds and trauma you were exposed to. Carl Jung defined the inner child as a sub-personality that can show up and take over who we are in the present moment. If we find ourselves being triggered with an emotion, it usually is something that goes deeper and is a byproduct of not feeling safe or feeling not enough. This can cause us to develop a deep sense of unworthiness.

As we are growing up, our paths and lives are usually carved out by our family's values and the way our parents believe and think. Most parents put kids in activities and sports that they feel best suits their needs, but these may not be what the child wants. Parents will unknowingly force their belief systems onto their children. I think most parents have the best intentions of their children at heart, but because they were taught that way, it's natural to parent the same way.

What happens, however, is a child starts to become conditioned into the path their parents want. If they don't perform the way their parents want them to, the parents may get upset. What happens then is that a conditional loving relationship develops, rather than an unconditional loving relationship. Most parents say they have unconditional love for their children, but sometimes that doesn't show in their actions, because they only reward the child with praise when the child does something they deem as "right." And if the child does something "wrong" or "not right," the response from the parents is wrapped up in shame. This results in a sense of unworthiness and guilt over not being enough.

This can happen with teachers and coaches, as well. This conditional love can really damage a child's sense of self, which will eventually lead to emotional outbursts and potential addiction or other unhealthy coping mechanisms down the line.

This happened often with my dad. Whenever I didn't play well in a hockey game or if I didn't bring home good grades, I was met with anger from him or the silent treatment. When I didn't meet his standards, he withheld his love. I didn't realize until later this came from a place of not having unconditional love for himself, which came from the way he was raised.

THEO FLEURY

When I think about trauma, one story immediately comes into my mind. It has always really impacted me and stuck out as being one of the most inspiring ones I have ever heard. Theo Fleury was one of my hockey idols growing up, and I had the privilege of having this guy on *University of Adversity.*

If you don't already know, Theo Fleury is a Stanley Cup champion, Olympic gold medalist, and a survivor of some of the most horrific trauma one can endure as a young man.

He was sexually abused by his coach, Graham James, as a young man in his junior hockey days. I remember reading his book, *Playing with Fire,* and just thinking about myself as a young athlete, what that was like, and how challenging it would have been if I had had to go through such a painful and disgusting experience. The things his coach did were unimaginable. This was someone whom this young athlete trusted; someone who was supposed to be looking out for his best interests.

Taking advantage of a child sexually, someone who is vulnerable, is literally the worst thing a human being can do. Theo was repeatedly sexually abused for many years. He discusses this painful experience in his book, and we talked about it on the podcast interview we had in late 2019.

Addiction is the byproduct of trauma, and alcohol was Theo's numbing agent. This eventually led to a lot of cocaine, which eventually led to his getting himself into trouble while he was playing professional hockey. This ultimately led to the end of his career. Theo's early journey represented a full-blown Distractor archetype.

Hearing his powerful story was extremely moving for me, because it takes a lot of courage, a lot of guts, a lot of bravery to share a story like this with the world. When he first came out and spoke about this in the late '90s, it was one of the first times anybody had ever really spoken about sex abuse in sports. Ever since I learned about this, I have admired him as a hero.

There is an element to sports culture, at least there was when I was younger, that it isn't okay to show weakness; it isn't okay to express your feelings. What Theo did was change the narrative on what was considered strength in sports, because if you are somebody who has something adverse in your life, some form of past trauma you're holding onto, that is only going to weaken you; it's not going to give you strength. What gives you strength is to be able to share your truth and vulnerability. When the darkest parts of you are exposed to the light, they can exit your body, mind, and identity.

Theo said in a podcast interview on my show, "You are only as sick as your secrets." That quote really hit home, because those secrets we hold in are like poison.

We aren't meant to do this thing alone, especially in dealing with trauma. Theo now continues to share his message and speak on stages around the world.

ERICK GODSEY

One of my mentors, someone from whom I have had the pleasure of learning and diving deeper into this concept over the last couple years, is fellow podcaster Erick Godsey.

His ability to articulate the entire concept of trauma is the best I've heard yet. I had him on my show specifically to give a masterclass on trauma for everyone, so my audience could have a better understanding of what it is and how to move through it. Check out the episode here.

ANGER: A SECONDARY EMOTION

Understanding anger is something I think all people can benefit from. You may think to yourself, *Well, I don't feel angry.* If this is you, then this section on anger is *for* you. Anger is one of these emotions we all feel from time to time or we greatly suppress it. After a while, that suppression becomes second nature.

Let's talk about what causes us to be angry. Why are some more angry than others? And why are some able to keep their calm?

I have noticed in my own life that anger has never served me well. Anger has always been my number-one weakness and is usually the emotion that gets me in the most trouble with the people I care about. There was a time when I thought that showing my anger and emotion was something that made me tough; or it signified that I cared or was passionate about a certain situation or really meant business, and what I was saying really mattered. I nearly wore my anger as a badge of honor.

What I've come to realize was just how unhelpful this was. My anger didn't help get to the root of any situation I was in and didn't help me express what actually needed to be expressed. Losing control, yelling, or anything else that expresses anger inappropriately like this is a weakness, not a strength.

Since I grew up in a very emotional family with a lot of fighting, I witnessed a lot of anger, so I naturally developed that as a natural response to events. When things went wrong, somebody got angry. And now, when I look back at myself, that was always the main go-to emotion that came up whenever some sort of discomfort or pain or embarrassment surfaced. But now, as I start to really understand what anger is, from my own research and from really going within myself to see what causes me to get angry, I've come to a lot of really interesting conclusions.

I came across this interesting theory of the Anger Iceberg created by the Gottman Institute. This theory asserts that the anger we show is just what we're seeing, the tip of the iceberg. Then, under the water—what you don't see—are the underlying, unprocessed emotions that cause anger. These emotions can include fear, shame, depression, embarrassment, insecurity, jealousy, and guilt. Therefore, anger is a secondary emotion, triggered by root trauma.

This is related to Sigmund Freud's iceberg theory regarding our conscious and unconscious minds. He asserted that five percent of our mind, the conscious mind, is above the surface of the water. This is what you can consciously recall and talk about. Ninety-five percent of our minds, however, are unconscious and underneath the surface of the water.

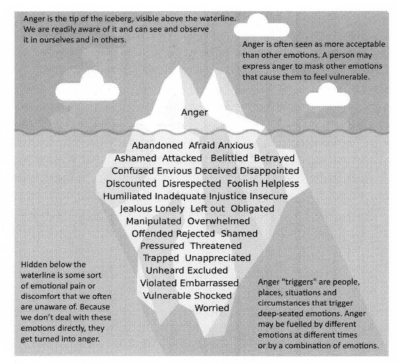

Anger is the tip of the iceberg, visible above the waterline. We are readily aware of it and can see and observe it in ourselves and in others.

Anger is often seen as more acceptable than other emotions. A person may express anger to mask other emotions that cause them to feel vulnerable.

Anger

Abandoned Afraid Anxious
Ashamed Attacked Belittled Betrayed
Confused Envious Deceived Disappointed
Discounted Disrespected Foolish Helpless
Humiliated Inadequate Injustice Insecure
Jealous Lonely Left out Obligated
Manipulated Overwhelmed
Offended Rejected Shamed
Pressured Threatened
Trapped Unappreciated
Unheard Excluded
Violated Embarrassed
Vulnerable Shocked
Worried

Hidden below the waterline is some sort of emotional pain or discomfort that we often are unaware of. Because we don't deal with these emotions directly, they get turned into anger.

Anger "triggers" are people, places, situations and circumstances that trigger deep-seated emotions. Anger may be fuelled by different emotions at different times or by a combination of emotions.

Image created by psychologist Claire Newton

Our subconscious minds are like the record-keepers of our lives; they keep track of everything, such as our memories and experiences, but we can't necessarily recall all of these memories and experiences or determine how they might be impacting us, particularly early memories like our childhood programming.

When we were children, we did not have a filter to decipher what was good versus what was bad when it came to our experiences, and many of them are stored in the subconscious mind. These experiences and interpretations lie below the surface of the water, and much of it will never be discovered. The problem is that a lot of our behaviors, emotions, and anger come from this under-the-surface stuff we're completely unaware of.

As we start to do more healing work and start to become more intuitive and connected with our conscious minds, more of our subconscious begins to surface. What's interesting is, when we do get traumatized and that anger surfaces, it's usually because the left side of the brain gets affected and becomes almost silenced. The right side, however, is enhanced. That causes these emotions to stir, and that's why people lose their temper or become super-emotional and react. The left side of their brain, the logical/analytical side, is affected by the right side taking over.

This is really important to be mindful of—often, when you get angry or even have a temper tantrum, it's just because something that is trauma-related has not been dealt with. Allowing ourselves and others to process anger is important. Often anger is perceived as "bad" when we are children, and it is emotion that fosters shame within us. Most if not all of us are learning how to process anger for the very first time as adults.

When you witness someone experiencing anger, it's important not to take these things as a personal attack, especially now that you know what lies beneath it. You can't control how that person feels, so it's important to understand that it has nothing to do with you and taking it personally just makes you the victim.

When someone is angry, it is important to understand that they are feeling the way they're feeling because they look at life through their lens and their stories, and they are doing their best to process their emotions. This can be tricky because it's easy to react and think it's your fault or that you should take it personally and feel bad about it. That's what most people in our society do when they witness anger. However, all that does is create more of the same thing: it creates more anger and it creates more stress.

This is something I experienced when I was growing up. If somebody in my family got angry, then that would cause the other person to take it personally and get angry back. Then, it would turn into a personal attack, back and forth. This happened my entire life: somebody's anger would get blamed on somebody else, and the other person would take it personally, and then it would never end. It can end when somebody can step back, be the bigger person, and not take it personally. This takes a certain amount of emotional intelligence, awareness, and understanding, but in dealing with our own anger and effectively dealing with someone else's, this is very, very important to understand.

When we understand this, we can process our anger and allow the other person to process theirs. When we can do this effectively, we come closer to understanding what is actually causing the trigger. This is a vital step in moving through adversity, since a lot of our perceived struggles are based on the outside world and other people's pain. We do not have to own this pain or carry the weight of it on our shoulders. When we learn why it is happening to ourselves and others, we can put this weight down and move through life light and free.

HEALING AND TRAUMA

If we don't process traumatic events when they happen (and we often don't), then those memories and feelings get stored as trauma. Trauma is like a kink in the timeline of your psyche. What happens is, in that moment where the emotion and feeling got stuck, the experience is never complete or resolved, so it starts to show up in other areas of your life later on as different emotions or feelings.

I like to think of trauma as kinks in your garden hose; every time there is a kink, it causes a disruption of flow in the water. The bigger the kink, the harder it is for the water to move through. This will create chaos in parts of the hose, and the hose itself will jump around, if the water can't flow properly. Our timelines and psyches are full of these kinks, and it's important for us to untangle this mess in order for life to flow smoothly.

As I continue on this path of transformation, I have realized the importance of trauma in our development and how it affects all of us in different ways. Sometimes, it's hard to wrap my head around why we need to experience trauma and suffering, but from studying the work of Gabor Maté, I have learned that it is that our job as human beings to learn through the suffering and adversity we face. When we can overcome the suffering and when we can get through the trauma and heal it, we can uncover the true beauty and essence of who we really are.

Trauma is a complex area, and there isn't a one-size-fits-all solution. A great first step, however, is to identify your triggers, connect with your inner child, and introspect on which of the adversity archetypes (Distractor, Victim, Fixer, and Warrior) tend to surface when you are triggered.

Go back to the previous chapter and look at the adversity archetypes again, but this time with a trauma-informed lens. In the chapters that follow, you will learn more tools for uncovering and overcoming trauma through my framework for overcoming adversity—the 5 A's.

CHAPTER 5

THE *5A'S*: A FRAMEWORK FOR MASTERING ADVERSITY

> *"The truth is that adversity is a part of most days. Whether you are ultimately weakened or strengthened by each event or the accumulation of events will depend on you first mastering the ability to Take It On!"*
> — Erik Weihenmayer, first blind person to reach the summit of Mount Everest

The 5A Framework is a tool you can apply whenever you experience adversity, whether it is a short-term crisis you find yourself in or a long-term challenge you are facing. This process happens internally and can occur in a matter of minutes, or it can take years, depending on who you are, what kind of adversity you are facing, and the tools you utilize to move through it. When you move through each of the five steps, or pillars, of this framework, you are working from a place of adversity toward understanding, unlocking, and becoming the Warrior archetype—the most empowered human you can possibly be in the position you're at with what you currently know.

This method is based on what has worked for me and my experience after taking an extensive deep dive into personal development and spirituality when I was tired of blindly facing adversity without having the right tools to move through it. Also, from speaking on my podcast, *University of Adversity*, to legendary people who have overcome massive challenges. It wasn't a process I deliberately developed—just something I noticed I had done many times over, to meet a challenge, overcome it, and create something beautiful from it. The most successful people I've met have done this, too; they may use different language to describe their experiences, but this is what I've distilled from the numerous hours I've spent with them—commonalities in the process of overcoming challenge.

The process begins with *Awareness* of your present circumstances; without awareness, there is no forward movement. You remain lost. When you *Accept* your circumstances as they are and are no longer in denial, it is easier to shift into a solution. In order to move toward embodying the Warrior, you must *Aspire* to become the best version of yourself; an identity shift must occur. You need a target in the distance to aim for. In order to be the person who has all of the success you desire and to manifest the result you want, you must *Align* your behaviors with that ideal. The last step, *Alchemize*, is when you bring it all together and use creative energy to bring something good from the adversity you're experiencing.

As you read through the five steps—Awareness, Acceptance, Aspire, Align, and Alchemize—and my stories that describe how I've mastered each of these pillars in different areas of my life, reflect on your own experience and how you can apply these steps to your unique circumstances. I have also included some of the practical tools that have helped me move through each pillar, which you can use in your everyday life.

THE ADVERSITY ANTIDOTES

Throughout this process, you're going to fall off. We all do. Remember the archetypes from Chapter 3? Well, the wounded archetypes—the Distractor, Fixer, and Victim—tend to pop up in our lives and knock us off the path to mastering the adversity we are facing. The behaviors these archetypes exhibit keep us stuck in adversity, and they will show their faces as you're going through these steps.

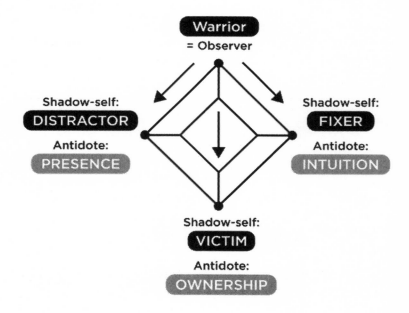

SHADOW ARCHETYPES AND ANTIDOTES

Shadow Archetype	**Antidote**
DISTRACTOR →	**Presence** • Meditation • Respond vs. react • Living in the now • Deep connection • Love vs. fear • Unattached to past & future
VICTIM →	**Ownership** • Takes responsibility • Practices gratitude • Awareness of triggers and their roots • Empowered • Release stories & limiting inherited beliefs • Resourcefulness • Empathic
FIXER →	**Intuition** • Self-trust/Self-love • Internal guidance • Acceptance of past • Feeling enough/Feeling whole • Comfort in uncertainty • Grounded

The Warrior observes all of the other archetypes—Fixer, Distractor, and Victim—and experiences all of their dark aspects. Since we can embody any one of these archetypes at any given time, we must ask ourselves, how do we get out of this archetype and back to Warrior energy? What is the antidote to these dark aspects of ourselves? Well, the answer is *light*. We live in a world of polarity, and we cannot have light without dark and vice versa. Each of the adversity archetypes has a specific antidote we can apply when we are experiencing it, which will move us out of the wounded archetype and toward the Warrior.

In the following chapters, you will learn more about each of the adversity antidotes and how to apply them. I will also provide examples from my experience in which I fell into the Distractor, Victim, and Fixer archetypes and how these specific antidotes—Presence, Ownership, and Intuition—helped move me back on my path to embody the Warrior.

MOVE OUT OF THE WOUNDED CYCLE, INTO THE HEALING CYCLE

The Wounded Cycle is a trap many of us fall into when we attempt to improve ourselves and overcome adversity. This is where we get stuck. A lot of us do try to work on ourselves—whether it's a health-related goal, finding a career that's more aligned with our interests and values, or bettering a relationship—and find we fall short for whatever reason. This sends us into the Wounded Cycle, where we go from embodying the Fixer to embodying the Victim for a period of time, ruminating over the perceived failure and blaming the perceived failure on factors outside of ourselves.

Uncomfortable with the emotions that this perceived failure brings up, we move into Distractor behaviors—drinking drugs, social media, television, etc.—in order to distance ourselves from these painful feelings. After some time has passed, we focus on "fixing" ourselves and our situations again with things outside of ourselves—whether it be with a new book, a new relationship, or a new experience. When this doesn't "work," we spiral back into the Wounded Cycle, and we keep perpetuating this cycle every time we encounter adversity.

THE WOUNDED CYCLE

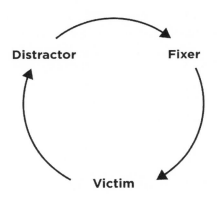

EXAMPLE: **Fixer** ➡ I'm going to prove myself! Oops, I failed.

Victim ➡ I'll never be good enough.

Distractor ➡ I'm going to go out and get drunk to avoid these uncomfortable feelings.

The Healing Cycle is the solution to the Wounded Cycle. When we find ourselves in the spiral of embodying the wounded archetypes, we must apply the specific antidote to get us back to embodiment of the Warrior. These specific antidotes–Presence, Ownership, and Intuition–shine light on our Distractor, Victim, and Fixer behaviors, respectively, and allow us to move back toward Warrior energy. The antidotes serve to transmute the low-vibration energy of discomfort we are feeling into a higher vibration. When we take ownership of the state of our lives, it allows us to accept what is and live in the moment, giving us the ability to cultivate a deeper sense of self, thereby harnessing our intuition and building deep trust in the future.

In the following chapters, I will go into detail about what each of these antidotes looks like in real-life situations, but for now, take a look at the antidotes and the Healing Cycle in the chart below, and keep this in mind as you read through the *5 A's* and learn about the adversity antidotes.

THE HEALING / WARRIOR CYCLE

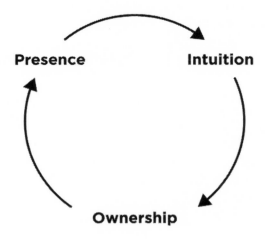

EXAMPLE: **Ownership** ➡ I accept and embrace my past and every decision I have made.

Presence ➡ I am able to connect with the present moment and appreciate where I am right here, right now.

Intuition ➡ I can now hear my innermost desires and beliefs and trust in my ability to make them a reality.

CHAPTER 6

STEP #1: AWARENESS

"By taking the time to stop and appreciate who you are and what you've achieved—and perhaps learned through a few mistakes, stumbles, and losses—you actually can enhance everything about you. Self-acknowledgment and appreciation are what give you the insights and awareness to move forward toward higher goals and accomplishments."

— Jack Canfield

Awareness is like a high-level, macro, nonjudgmental view of your life; being able to look at your way of being objectively. You have an understanding of where you are today, how you got there, and why you are the way you are. Awareness is seeing with clear vision the many decisions made along the way that led to where you are now.

It's important to identify those choices in order to clearly see the unique path you're on. If you don't know where you've come from, then it's impossible to know where you're going, because you don't have an understanding of who you are.

The book *Awareness* by Anthony de Mello had a profound effect on my personal development journey. In it, de Mello asserts you come either from love or from fear.

When I read that, it completely changed my life. You can look at your decisions and your choices and ask yourself, "Is this coming from love? Or is this coming from fear?"

This isn't a question you ask your mind; it's more about how you are feeling in your body. The body always knows. That is the simplest way to look at it. Fear is egoic. Fear is based on shame, judgment, resentment, and anger. Love is based on joy, playfulness, wholeness, happiness, and gratitude. When you're aware of how you make your decisions, then you can literally change your life.

This simple question has taught me how to stop, take a breath, and decide whether or not I want to move forward in a decision or action. It has kept me from acting out of my trauma and ego. It has kept me from posting a lot of shit online that I would have posted in the past! It stops me from reacting.

Now, I ask myself, "How would the best version of me, the person I truly admire, respond to this?" Now, I can always respond from a place of love.

"A RUDE AWAKENING"—EMBODYING THE DISTRACTOR

In December 2015, at thirty-two years old, I suddenly jolted out of bed from a puddle of sweat. I was shaking with panic and anxiety.

How could it possibly be time to wake up? I thought to myself. Sitting in a tiny little cardboard box of an apartment in Bondi Beach, Australia, I recalled the night before and the punishment I'd put my body through. The sense of regret and shame coursed through my body as I thought about the amount of alcohol and drugs I'd had the night before, which had led me to this moment...

Here's the truth... This was a typical weekend. On a typical weekend, my night would consist of a steady flow of booze coupled with a steady flow of caffeine and, possibly on top of that, a couple lines of coke later in the evening. What I couldn't believe about Australia was how open everyone was about drugs and partying. Literally everyone partied *hard;* it was almost like a rite of passage. To be honest, these typical weekends were some of the wildest and most fun nights of my life, but they came with a heavy price.

I would spend the night in and out of the busy bar, making drinks, running around, flirting with the ladies, and making sure people were getting their food and drinks. I had to go up and down stairs and elevators to help the busy bar downstairs, juggling all of these tasks while trying to keep a steady buzz going and remain functional and coherent. I became a master at the balancing act of being able to know when I needed more booze, when I needed water, food, coffee, or a line of coke.

The coke wasn't always around, but when it was, it was a free-for-all. I would run out of the bar to a bathroom where a guest had left some for me, up to a room in the hotel, down the back stairwell, or to a secret storage floor called 2F, where a lot of crazy shit went down. It was fucking nuts, and it would go on like that right up until we closed at 2:00 or 3:00 a.m., and sometimes even way after we closed, depending on the night.

I would always make it a point to take a short, forty-five-minute break mid-shift, around 6:00 p.m., when things were a bit calm. With one of the servers from the bar, we'd go to another nearby bar. The usual protocol was a shot of tequila and slamming a couple of daiquiris. We would head back to work nice and lit up, ready for the second half of the night.

The night would always unfold with more chaos, and then it would be a mad scramble to close up the bar, cash out the registers, and get out as fast as we could, so we could make it to the Smoking Panda, which was a late-night bar open until 6:00 a.m. The chaos and debauchery always sucked me in, as I was immediately greeted with a cocktail and a shot. All of the bartenders and hospitality staff from across the city went there. The Central Business District (CBD) in Sydney had enforced a lockdown, where no one could enter a bar after 1:30 a.m. This pub was one of the only places allowed to stay open.

This specific night was no different than the rest of those typical weekend nights...

At work, we'd had some massive Christmas parties, so the booze, music, and vibes were flowing. The guests were offering us drugs, and the staff were running around all over, fucked up out of their minds. The DJ was blasting great tunes, and other staff who had gotten off work at the restaurant were at the bar, drinking. It was pure craziness. The amount of alcohol consumed was ridiculous, and the feeling and taste of cocaine was still stuck in my nose the next day.

We went hard, and once we closed the bar, it was game on. As usual, we hit the Smoking Panda. I ended up downing some classic daiquiris, an old fashioned, perhaps a Negroni, or maybe a dirty gin martini or two, and several shots of tequila. After that, I don't remember what I drank. I drank there until 6:00 a.m. when it closed.

A few of us made our way down to the pub that opened at 6:00 a.m. This was always a wild scene, because all the tradies, construction workers, city workers, and anyone else who worked all night would come for a knock-off drink. It was as if the party was starting at 6:00 a.m. We sat and smashed Jager bombs and ciders and popped an MDMA pill or two until the wee hours of 10:00 a.m., also known as stupid o' clock. We just bounced around the early morning like lunatics until I finally looked at my phone and saw the time.

There comes a point when you know you have to stop... and this was it. I started to think about the day ahead of me, but I didn't worry too much. I thought to myself, *I will just grab some McDonald's* (or macas, as they call it in Australia), *take it home in an Uber, and eat. I will make sure I get at least three hours of sleep, and I'll be fine...* Famous last words...

Back to the morning, or rather that afternoon...

I picked up my phone, praying I could get another hour of sleep and hoping that I didn't fuck anything up at work the night before. I realized going back to sleep wasn't an option.

Sickness and panic flowed through my entire body as I peeled my corpse out of the pool of sweat. As I stood up, I looked at the loud, buzzing fan in front of me and felt a light breeze on my sweaty body. Noticing the old, '70s-looking red-and-orange paint that had been stripped off the walls in my beat-up little cardboard box of an apartment, I said to myself, "How the fuck am I going to do this?"

My heart raced. I smelled the disgusting odor of McDonald's from the night before, and then I could taste it in my mouth. McChicken and Big Mac wrappers and boxes of chicken nuggets covered the coffee table to my right. "How is it even possible that you have to work?" I asked myself again.

I felt like I hadn't slept a wink. My mouth felt like I was swallowing sandpaper. My body shook as I wobbled to the bathroom. I could feel there was still alcohol in my system and knew that the only way to get rid of this horrendous headache, which felt like hammers chipping away at my skull, was to have a drink.

I made my way to the freezer and took out the ice-cold vodka, disgusted with what I had become. As soon as I drank the syrupy, ice-cold liquid, I started to feel a sense of warmth through my body—like a warm hug of comfort.

It was now 1:10 p.m., and I had to be at work at 2:00. *I have to shower, call an Uber, and make it through the crazy Bondi Beach traffic to get to work on time...*

Once again, I thought about the night before, trying to remember if I'd fucked anything up and praying that I hadn't. I looked through the messages on my phone and didn't see anything from my boss or the hotel night team, so it was safe to assume I was okay. Still... the deep anxiety invaded my body like a pile of bricks being dropped on my chest.

In the bathroom, I sat on the toilet, crouched over, with my hands on my head, thinking, *How long am I going to keep doing this?*

It was only Saturday. I had another twelve-hour shift to get through, and this would be my third night in a row when I'd had to power through and somehow balance myself, so I could operate and function without losing control. I hopped in the shower, turned on the freezing-cold water, and forced my lifeless body awake.

I started to feel a sense of semi-aliveness, but tears rolled down my face as I let out a deep yawn. I thought about how badly I needed a *massive coffee* to send a jolt of caffeine into my fragile, exhausted body. Tears continued to roll down my face.

I am so fucking tired. How am I going to do this? I just kept thinking about how challenging this was going to be. But I reminded myself that I'd done it before and could do it again. *I just need to power through.*

I started to panic that I would be late as I waited for the Uber driver to accept my call. Finally, when he did, I saw that I would arrive at work late, at 2:10 p.m. As I headed outside into the blazing hot sun, in the 95-degree heat on a sweltering Sydney Saturday afternoon, I thought, *Okay... Not a big deal. I will just sneak in as fast as I can, down a bit of food from the staff cafeteria, grab my cash float, and make it look like I've been there for a while. I can't let them know I'm still half asleep. I have to try to hide the scent of alcohol sweating out every pore of my body...*

I knew I would pull it off as I always did, but I still felt this deep feeling of panic in my gut and in my chest. The reality of the situation was that it didn't really matter if I was late, because I was a manager. What I was really worried about was if I'd made any mistakes the night before. I always felt this dread that maybe my boss saw me drinking or I'd fucked up something with the cash. I knew I'd always managed to do the job properly, but I couldn't help but feel a sense of panic, amplified by the lack of sleep and the hangover. I knew then that I had to make sure everything was done correctly with the setup or I'd never hear the end of it. My anxiety rose to extreme levels, and I started to think of all the worst-case scenarios as shame riddled my entire body.

The Uber arrived, and I jumped in. I couldn't take my eyes off my phone, continuing to panic about being late. As we wove in and out of traffic, I kept thinking about my plan when I got to work. My stomach rumbled from both sickness and hunger. I started to get impatient with how long it was taking to get there. Every red light we hit, I worried more, but I tried to control my anxiousness and not lose my shit.

When I finally arrived at the hotel, I started a light jog in my tight skinny jeans, my sweaty button-up shirt, and blazer, along with my uncomfortable shoes that dug into the backs of my feet. I ran through the back alley to the door and went inside.

I hopped in the elevator nearby and headed up to the main floor and to the front office, where I needed to grab my float. *Here we go,* I thought. *Let's see if anyone says anything to me.*

The front desk was busy with check-ins, as usual, so I went into the back office to ask one of the shift managers to grab my float. No one said anything about the night before, and I felt a sense of relief. *Thank God.* I tried not to get too close or breathe on anyone, because I knew I still probably smelled like alcohol.

I was a bit dizzy as I signed out my float and headed back to the elevator to get to my bar upstairs. I was feeling super rough at this point—tired and a bit sick— but I knew I had to keep going. Normally, I would go to the back cooler and grab something in there or I'd just unwrap one of the bottles at the bar and pour myself a sneaky one, but this time, I said fuck it and just went to the bar and poured myself a triple Belvedere vodka– and down the hatch. It was warm and gross, but it was like medicine, and I felt alive again. I felt a sense of energy flow in. Now all I needed was a strong coffee.

With a big smile on my face, I walked down the stairs to the main bar and the restaurant on my right. The restaurant was busy with the aftermath of a Christmas lunch, and the main bar was rocking with a wedding party. Everyone was enjoying the festive season. *Thank God I don't have to deal with that right now,* I thought as I set up the bar upstairs.

I walked over to the espresso machine and made myself four shots of espresso, dumped a splash of cold milk in there.... and *boom*! I was back! I felt like myself again. I had made it through the first part of personal hell that I'd put myself through... at least, for now.

I thought to myself, *I wonder what is going to happen tonight? What kind of fucking craziness am in for?*

***

I tell this story to illustrate the insanity of my day-to-day and how I was literally embodying the Distractor archetype in every aspect of my life. What I realize now is that I was in so much pain and I lacked confidence and self-worth. The only way I could deal with those feelings was through creating this identity that involved alcohol and partying.

Living this lifestyle made it very easy to numb myself, because my entire job was partying and giving people a great experience. I didn't have to feel and face the deeper issues that came from my trauma and deep-rooted pain.

Not only was I distracting myself with alcohol, my entire purpose and self-worth came from getting validation from women. If I could distract myself and numb myself with alcohol, then I'd have the confidence to go after the girl and distract myself from being alone, because my attention and energy would be on her. I received so much validation from these behaviors and working in bars that it was hard to see how it wasn't actually serving my greater good.

I distracted myself with alcohol and with women for many years, because I didn't know how to cope with feeling like who I was wasn't enough. We see this happen a lot in our society: people not only distract themselves from reality with alcohol and validation from other people, but with food, their phone, or anything else that takes them out of feeling the feelings of discomfort in the present moment.

When we seek short-term pleasure, we sacrifice long-term satisfaction and fulfillment. Distracting ourselves in the present moment will only lead to longer-term suffering and move us further away from connecting to our truths.

The Distractor archetype is very important to be aware of because we all fall into this category at some time or another. The goal isn't to be perfect but to be aware when we are numbing ourselves. When we realize we are embodying this archetype, we must question what characteristics we are projecting and what we are diverting ourselves from feeling.

PRESENCE: THE ANTIDOTE FOR THE DISTRACTOR

"When you are present without the conditioning of your past, you become the presence of God."

— Eckhart Tolle

This quote is a powerful representation of what presence looks like—a connection to God, to the Universe—once we are free of the diversions and distractions of our past stories. This connection allows you to get out of your head and into your heart; into a place of love and out of a place of fear.

One story I'd like to share before diving into the importance of presence is about when I actually discovered what presence meant.

For a few years, I found myself reading books that really didn't serve me. Mostly, these were depressing biographies of rockstars or pro athletes who spoke about their reckless lifestyles and what came from it. Although entertaining, I always felt depleted afterward. Their stories hit on all my deepest fears and anxieties and left me in a very negative state. I'd ask myself, "Why am I reading this? Why am I not reading things that make me feel good?"

So, for whatever reason, I was called to read *The Power of Now* by Eckhart Tolle. That changed everything for me and opened the door to many other books, which eventually led me to a consistent meditation practice and to adopting a new perspective for how to look at life.

I started to get an understanding of what *NOW* meant and how now, aka presence, is all we actually have. When we are depressed, we are living in the past; when we are anxious, we are living in the future; but when we are present, we don't feel anything but what is right in front of us. It took me a while to wrap my head around this concept, but once I got it, it was powerful. That was really the start of my personal development journey—when I felt the freedom of what presence meant.

So, how does this concept of presence relate to the Distractor archetype? Well, when we are distracting ourselves, we are avoiding presence, because we are avoiding potential discomfort in the present moment. We find something to take us out of that feeling of discomfort, and sometimes we don't even know it's happening. The Distractor is looking for a solution outside of himself or herself to numb the pain, escape, or avoid feeling those present-moment feelings.

We can shift from the Distractor to the Warrior when we focus on going inward and experience detachment and inner connectedness, not thinking about past or future but focusing on right now.

Moving out of the Distractor and into presence doesn't just happen when you are by yourself; it also happens with others. How often do you find yourself in a group or with friends, where people *aren't* on their phones or looking for the next thing? In general, we have so much stimulation and so many options, it is easy to be a Distractor. The same thing can happen on a date. It's a terrible feeling to look over, when you're on a date, and see the other person on their phone, but that is usually a sign that they are insecure and afraid to feel the present moment or have a challenging conversation.

Witnessing this from a Warrior's perspective is so important, because you are essentially taking your life back and all the feelings it brings. It's important to feel all of the feelings the present moment has, whether they make you happy or uncomfortable. There is always a lesson in the present moment, and the best gift you can offer yourself or anyone around you is presence—a very powerful characteristic of the Warrior spirit and energy.

Stepping out of a distraction, which usually comes from a place of fear, requires the energy of love and full acceptance of the present moment, as well as an awareness of when you are distracting. Being in control of your impulses and behaviors puts you in the driver's seat when it comes to bringing more presence to your life.

CULTIVATING AWARENESS THROUGH PRESENCE

When we begin to cultivate awareness of where we are in the present moment and why we are experiencing challenges, we have to be aware of our pasts and think about the times when we acted out of fear. When we get a clear understanding of the choices we made, then we can say, "All right, here we go. I've learned. I've assessed what I've done—the good, the bad, and the ugly. And now, all there is is the present moment I am in right now."

Being aware and having that perspective is the only way for you to ever begin to change, because from awareness comes an understanding, an acceptance. Once you have that awareness, you can ask yourself: "How do I move forward? What's holding me back? What are the emotions that stem from past trauma?"

In order to get a deeper understanding, you can ask yourself: "What is it that throws me off? What makes me feel good?"

If you don't have awareness, you'll never know that, and you'll never be able to change course. It's all about asking yourself the right questions rather than just reacting. This is the first step to awareness—putting an end to living on autopilot.

In my own life, I've had to go back and think about the timeline of the decisions I made, why I made them, and their potential outcomes. There are not many things in my past that I'm really proud of. I made a lot of mistakes. However, on the larger scale of things, I did listen to whether or not something felt right when it came to big, life-altering decisions. I usually was pretty good at tapping into my intuition. It's essential to have an understanding of your behaviors as well as your strengths and weaknesses, without judgment. If you want to make a change, you have to be able to look at the whole picture.

A huge part of my journey to finding greater awareness was coming to terms with the fact that I reacted so strongly out of my fear of abandonment because of all the loss I've experienced in my life, from having to move across the country away from my mother, to losing my brother to suicide, to losing my dad to cancer, among other family members. I discovered that, whenever I got close to somebody, at some point, I would begin to retreat, sabotage the relationship, or create a block between us, because I feared that I would ultimately lose them.

It was important for me to be aware of this, because if I'm not aware of those things that trigger me, I'm never going to be able to fix them or heal.

THE IMPACT OF OUR VICES

Some people are so lost in showing up how they think they are supposed to, they don't understand where they are masking their truth. So, they just take medication or numb themselves with their vices. This is something I did for a long time, and I refuse to do it anymore.

Part of awareness is understanding what clouds it. It's the way we treat our bodies and our minds that makes all the difference. It's the choices we make that distract or heal us. It's our sleep, our food, our body movement, and our ability to detach from what is unhealthy for us. It's allowing ourselves to *feel* things so we can move through the body sensations that accompany them.

Because we do not live in a world that encourages us to sit with our feelings, when we attempt this, it is easy to run when it gets hard. It's not fun to face our demons and to sit through pain, but the only way your body can get familiar with that sensation is by connecting to that awareness. For so many years, I masked the truest parts of myself with alcohol, and the days that followed would be a roller coaster ride of complete anxiety.

You're not going to be able to move forward if you don't have a full understanding of all the darkness that still lives within you. When you're leaning on those vices, you're just further numbing your awareness, taking away the true essence of your soul. Your intuition, your inner knowing, is meant to feel.

Sometimes, it's going to give you things that are unpleasant. It's not always sunshine and rainbows. It doesn't always bring you opportunities. Sometimes, however, it's the short-term discomfort that eventually brings you the long-term fulfillment and happiness.

ACCOUNTABILITY & AWARENESS

If you're constantly numbing yourself with distractions, you're not going to hear the whisper—your intuition. The whisper gets louder, and you'll get stuff thrown at you, but you still won't pay attention. The Universe will then start to yell at you and shake you until you listen. Adversity is the punch in the face we sometimes need to make a much-needed change. Cultivating awareness within ourselves helps to soften the blow and helps us act before things get harder.

So many people think others are out to get them or think it's someone else's fault that they're experiencing adversity. If you think like this, you're too busy letting your external environment and everybody around you dictate your life. You're not being accountable. You're not listening to the whisper. You're not even allowing yourself to listen.

Listening to it is hard; I get it. It's not easy being human. We learn through pain. We grow through pain. It has a purpose, I promise. The trauma and the painful experiences are the building blocks for us to discover who we really are.

As humans, we learn through these moments of suffering. It's hard. Gabor Maté says, if we understand the beauty behind trauma, once it's healed, it reveals this magic within you. Nobody chooses to experience trauma, so the stuff we go through might be part of what we're supposed to do. The beauty of healing is that it reveals so much; it's the doorway to our true essence.

We're all destined for greatness. That's why we were born. But there's a lot of stuff we need to figure out along the way. That's the human experience. It's not good or bad; it just is. And it's important to feel these things. It's important to have an understanding that it's essential we go through things sometimes, but it's more essential that we learn the lesson.

Hitting rock bottom after my crazy lifestyle of drinking, partying, and wearing my body out was really how I began to step into awareness. I woke up and thought, *Is this all there is?* I knew I was meant for more. But I knew I needed some form of guidance.

I was a big fan of inspiration—not motivation, inspiration. People's stories and the concept of the hero's journey really resonated with me. That's why I started my show. It really inspired me when someone was able to beat the odds and do something great. When the picture of what was possible was painted for me, that's what made me take a good hard look at my life and step into my own awareness of what I had created and why I had created it. And, of course, it motivated me to heal and do better for myself.

I always was really interested in people who were doing great things. People like Tony Robbins, Tim Ferriss, Dr. Mercola, Dave Asprey, and Joe Rogan. I was always interested in becoming optimal, even though I drank a lot. I was very passionate about health and wellness. People used to call me a hypocrite because I'd be partying, but then I'd be taking care of myself eating healthy, juicing, and exercising.

I started to just pay attention to the things that made me feel shitty and the things that made me feel good at the simplest level. I was always able to navigate what felt good and what didn't; which people made me feel good and which ones didn't. I began following podcasts and listening to thought leaders. Finally, I stepped into the awareness that I was scared to live my life, like *truly* live my life full out. I was in fear because I had failed so much before, and I felt like such a loser at times.

When I really started to understand that alcohol and drugs and late nights were a factor in that, I knew it all had to go. I wanted to understand who I truly was, and those things were getting in the way. What I began to uncover was that I always knew I was going to be great, ever since I was a young kid playing hockey. I knew, after putting my body and my life through the wringer, that I needed to do something different, something that would serve humanity. It was my calling. Over the past three years, for the first time, I have felt like I'm actually living a meaningful life and helping people. And I wouldn't have gotten here without stepping into my own awareness and allowing it to show me what needed to change.

I think there's a point where we feel the weight of battling two identities. For so long, I was at a crossroads of these two versions of myself, and ultimately, I needed to choose, or I was going to rip in half. It was too much to keep going as both people.

I'd say to the false version of myself, *You've had dinner. You've stayed too long. It's time to go. You're overstaying your welcome.* That's literally what happened: I told the bartender party dude that he'd overstayed his welcome. But when I allowed myself to strip away all the layers, I realized that bartender party dude is just the inner child. Then, instead of telling him to go away, I began to ask myself, *What does this guy, this inner child, want?*

This is something we all battle to an extent, and it's an important part of awareness—recognizing our false identity is just the suppressed emotions and unmet needs we didn't receive as children. This bartender party dude needed to be seen and validated over and over and over again. An endless cycle, until I woke up to the fact that this was not who I actually am at my core.

I want to be clear: a lot of blessings came from my experience in the bar industry and my false identity in this world. It led me to discovering who I truly am. The hangovers sucked, and the feeling like shit sucked, but it brought me to now. It highlighted all my wounds, so I could stop masking them and finally begin to heal them. And for that I am in full gratitude and wouldn't change a thing.

THE UNRAVELING OF THE MIND LOOP

We live in the age of information, where distractions are coming at us a mile a minute, so a huge part of awareness is becoming conscious of what we're allowing our brains to consume. When you see something or absorb something and you suddenly feel triggered, it can bring on the thoughts that maybe you're not doing enough or maybe someone else has it more figured out than you or maybe you're lacking in some way. Then you start to question other things in your business, in your life, in the people around you, everything that you're doing, and start to doubt that you will be able to make the progress you desire.

This is where we can get into a spiral. We feel like what we're doing just isn't working. This happens because we think we should know exactly how things should be. We leave the present moment the minute we start to imagine scenarios, start to imagine the times when we made mistakes, the reasons things didn't work out before, and then we project that into the now and into the future, instead of just being present and knowing that the thoughts we're having right now are usually because of our current emotional state.

We need to be mindful of when we start to go into this downward spiral. If you feel it happening, ask yourself, "How do I feel in my body? Is what I am thinking true? Or is it a projection of fear, perhaps based on a past trauma?"

We live in this delusional world where we think everyone else has it figured out and we don't know what the fuck is going on. But that's not true. If you continue to believe this bullshit story, it's just going to create these spirals of shame and feelings that are going to keep you from the energetic vibration you need to be at.

I've experienced these spirals of self-doubt; where I doubt that what I'm doing is working. For example, when somebody reschedules a podcast interview, I might start to doubt they even wanted to do it. And then I might have thoughts like, *Well, maybe my podcast sucks. Maybe my brand sucks. Maybe everything I'm doing sucks... What am I doing?*

And then I start to think like that in other areas of my life. This is the spiral we can go into, if we're not careful, if we do not have awareness. If you allow the outside to take you over, you won't step into your greatest gifts, and you will deny the world of your greatest self. It will block you from all the impact, success, and fulfillment that are your birthright, all because you failed to be conscious to the manipulation of the outside world.

It's okay to trip up—it happens to all of us—but start to recognize it and change course. The people who succeed are able to quiet that sound. They're able to re-calibrate, re-energize, and re-focus on the things that serve them rather than the things that don't.

CONSCIOUS HEALING

There are plenty of modalities for this healing journey, and these are different for everyone. It's important to identify what those are for you, and it's important to have people whom you follow who can help you embody the characteristics that will empower you to live a great life.

The best leaders are the ones who are able to show you that you have it all within you; you just need to believe in yourself. In order to believe in yourself and to build your confidence, you need to be aware of all the things you do on a daily basis, all the things you don't want to do anymore, all the things you may not have been aware of, and then decide how you do want to show up.

And if you continue on this journey and you realize that the old stories keep showing up and the same people keep coming into your life, the same shitty situations, well, then it's time to ask yourself, "How can I heal this? What part of me needs healing? And why do I keep attracting this stuff?"

But you won't know that unless you're aware of what you do! And then, once you are aware of what you need to heal, you can reach out and find the resources and mentors who can help.

In addition to finding mentors, psychedelics can be useful for moving into greater awareness. As we discussed in Chapter 4, there are a lot of things we don't even know about ourselves, because they are buried in our subconscious. Psychedelics, if you go deep enough with them, will show you what you need to see—and sometimes *don't* want to see. That's why psychedelics can be powerful. You don't choose what you get to see. This can be difficult, because it forces people to look at things they may not want to look at, but, in turn, these medicines will lead to a greater level of awareness and healing.

There are exercises we can utilize to go back in our timeline to see what causes our Distractor patterns and triggers. Expressive writing is a tool by James Pennebaker that is so helpful. I was introduced to this through Erick Godsey's journaling course, *Make Your Myth,* which is absolutely profound.

Expressive writing is about writing without limitations like punctuation, grammar, or judgment. You do it for four days, for about twenty minutes per day, in a stream-of-consciousness style. This free-writing exercise forces you to dig into memories and traumas you haven't spoken about. It can get super dark, but it's important to process what comes up, because you're letting emotions fulfill their full cycle—part of that cycle being the awareness of how your past is dictating your future. You can't fix a problem if you don't know it is there.

I want to leave you with a super-easy first step for cultivating presence and awareness. Take control of your morning to fill your cup before you start your day. Start your day with presence, rather than reaching for your phone.

Every day, I have a morning routine that programs my mind and body for a good day before I reach for my phone. I have found, if I start my days this way, I am less reactive and less distractable.

My morning routine consists of reading, breathwork, meditation, and journaling. I have found, when I start my days this way, the phone can be used as a tool, not a distraction and not as a device that controls my behaviors. It's a simple technique but such a powerful way to change your relationship with technology.

Try it out for yourself! See if you can keep your phone on airplane mode until you've set the right tone for your day.

Getting into a conscious routine is a powerful way to program your mind, body, and spirit for the day, and it will become a lot easier to stay present. You will feel fewer impulses to distract yourself when you go inward and reflect first thing in the morning, with journaling, meditation, moving your body, or breathwork. Simple practices like these ones help you stay focused throughout the day, and it will get easier and easier the more you commit to it.

CHAPTER 7

STEP #2: ACCEPTANCE

"We cannot change anything unless we accept it."
— Carl Jung

One of the most intriguing aspects of philosopher Friedrich Nietzsche's ideas is his repeated fervor for a concept he called *amor fati*, translated from Latin as "a love of one's fate," or, said another way, a resolute, enthusiastic acceptance of everything that has happened in one's life.

Our society has been conditioned to embrace only things that feel good and to push away the things that feel bad. The problem is, when you don't accept the dark side of life, the things that sometimes don't feel as good, the darker parts of ourselves that we aren't proud of and the situations in the world that challenge us, then we are essentially denying part of ourselves. This is the reason becoming conscious of our shadow is so important.

Our human tendency is to focus on one side, which is the positive aspect of life, and to ignore the negative side, which is the darkness of our lives. When we do that, we become one-sided and out of touch with our truth. Our drive is to be good and only embrace goodness, because this is what was rewarded when we were children. This programming runs deep and causes us to reject critical pieces of ourselves. But all this does is suppress the darkness; it doesn't make it disappear. From seeking only the goodness in our lives, we become one-sided.

The idea here isn't to become darkness but to embrace it and learn to love it so it no longer has power over us. When we embody the darkness as part of our unique makeup and part of our story, then and only then can we become whole and the truest version of ourselves. It's not good or bad, but, for us to be whole, we need to embrace the dark *and* the light.

There is a huge misconception that, in order to explore the dark, you have to become the dark. Accepting things for what they are, not good or bad but the truth of reality, and learning to love all parts of yourself will simply allow you to bring more light to the darkness, which allows the darkness to have less control over your life. What we resist persists. The more we deny parts of ourselves, the more fragmented we become. Again, this isn't about becoming the darkness; this is about being able to love your imperfections because they are part of you. It's only "bad" because we decide that it is based on conditioning, fear, and ego.

As you continue to learn about adversity throughout this book, you will discover that the challenges you face in your life are always going to benefit you in some way, even though it's not easy to see in the moment. Whether it's good or bad, we must embrace it, we must allow it to breathe, and we must allow ourselves to accept whatever it is. This can be uncomfortable, but the discomfort will pass.

The problem is we don't learn about this stuff growing up, and we are conditioned to feel shame around things that don't go with the overarching narrative of the world we're living in. If it creates any sort of resistance or discomfort, it is considered negative, and we want to compartmentalize it and not deal with it. This only causes whatever we are avoiding to continue to grow and build on itself. If it's not processed, it will show up in another area of your life. Another very on-point quote from Carl Jung states, "Until you make the unconscious conscious, it will guide your life, and you will call it fate."

Amor fati is a beautiful term to embrace all that is—even the stuff that doesn't feel good—because, when that uncomfortable moment passes, there will always be a lesson. There will always be something positive from it.

To be able to see complete love for ourselves is our ability to see love in the world. That's why it's so important for us to work on unconditionally loving ourselves. This is the whole point of spirituality and religion—to work toward unconditional love. Unless you're Jesus or you're some spiritual master, you will spend your whole life trying to get to that point, but isn't it a great mission regardless? Isn't that a great goal—to be able to develop unconditional love for yourself and the people around you? It means embracing everything that is. As hard as it is to understand and acknowledge the chaos of the world and what's going on, we have to look at it from an empowered perspective and understand that this is happening for us, not to us, even though it doesn't look or feel like it sometimes. There will always be a lesson that we will learn and grow from.

Whether you believe that or not, I believe that every single one of us chose to be here. You're here for a reason. We don't really embrace the miracle that it is for us to be here as humans, to be able to live in bodies and create. If we really sit back and think about it—that we are conscious and are constantly shaping and creating this world, and that we can think and act on all of the amazingness we have—it's an absolute miracle. But we don't ever sit and think about this kind of stuff.

A lot of people think we're just here by accident; that there's no point. But I don't believe that. From my own journey of spiritual growth, from my own journey of working on myself and my spirituality, I've realized that we are more than just people who came here to work and die. There's more to us, there's more purpose, and that is really the goal: to develop and figure out what that is.

So, embrace it all, celebrate the wins, accept the challenges, and create a unique dance with yourself and the pain that you face in your life, so you can work with it and use it as a tool to propel you forward. When you are able to change the way you see things and you are able to look at them from a place of empowerment, complete ownership, then what you would see in front of you will change. The acceptance and embracing of all that is makes it so much easier.

But being able to sit in discomfort, being able to sit in moments that don't feel great without distracting yourself with some external thing or circumstance is a real skill; it's the Warrior in you. You are here for a reason. We are resilient. We have the ability to be able to come back to center after we get knocked down. We have to be able to embrace all of it as being perfect and beautiful. It's not easy when we're faced with it in the moment, and that's okay. It's part of the human experience. We must feel all of it, the motions, the good, the bad, the ugly, and then we must process it, allowing it a seat at the table, so you can get to know it and feel it. That way, it no longer becomes something that you resist; instead, it becomes something you always choose to love.

A MOTHER'S LOVE

As far as I can remember, I always loved the feeling of being desired by the opposite sex. As a kid, I remember feeling more valuable knowing that the girls liked me. I think that is pretty common among most kids and teenagers.

I started to really crave this feeling of being chosen, especially in my teen years after having to leave my mom behind. Because of the deep pain and sadness that I felt, missing my mom and after not being able to receive her nurturing and affection, I started to seek it in other places—with the opposite sex.

When you are raised with so much closeness and love from your mother, you become accustomed to the warm, nurturing feelings that love provides. When my parents divorced, that feeling was taken away, and I felt the subconscious urge to seek it out elsewhere. I didn't know it at the time, but looking back at my life, that is exactly what was happening.

In 1995, after leaving my mom behind and moving across the country, I experienced a deep, dark sadness. The only time I felt somewhat validated was when a hot girl at school had a crush on me, because, after my parents' divorce, I didn't feel wanted at all.

I started to get addicted to that feeling, and as I got older, I found myself wanting serious relationships, because I wanted to replace that love I rarely received as a teenager. My mom lived so far away, and sometimes it would be over a year between visits. Looking back, it seems as though every time I got into a relationship, I was almost looking for a mother-like figure, and I craved affection. In all of my relationships,

I desired a woman who would do my laundry and cook for me, all of the domestic acts in the house, and someone who would stay very close to me. It fulfilled that nurturing aspect that was absent throughout the latter half of my formative years.

The connection between my experience and what I looked for and was attracted to was completely unconscious. It's hard for me to talk about this because it's very personal, but it's the truth. As men (and women even), we need a mother's love, and if we don't get what we need from our mothers, we will seek it in the opposite sex. Through a lot of healing work and connecting the dots, I've learned why I tend to be closed off in relationships—because I stopped receiving this nurturing love from the one source it originally comes from.

In addition to choosing partners who had these nurturing qualities, I also started to notice the strong level of attachment I had in a relationship. I would often find myself being needy and opening up a bit sooner than I should have. This wasn't just the emotional component of wanting attention and validation from my partner; this was also sexually and in the validation that came from being seen and desired. The intensity this would create within the relationship dynamic often caused a rift with my partner, and my efforts would backfire, which resulted in me closing my heart. Whenever I felt my relationship was in jeopardy, it was as if I was reliving that same feeling of getting close to someone and then their leaving. It was a reopening of that same wound I'd suffered when I had to leave my mom so many years ago and a story that I've spent decades overcoming.

Eventually, I became a pro at closing my heart. After getting my heart broken the first time, I became very good at being able to separate sexual and physical desires from romantic attachment and commitment. For years, relationships became almost like a game to me. No matter whom I met or how I felt, they were *not* getting in my heart. I was like a rock and had no emotion toward the opposite sex most of the time. I still have times when I close my heart, even to this day. It is something I am continually working on.

My first real heartbreak, when I was seventeen, devastated me. I remember the deep sickness in my stomach, like I had been kicked in the gut, and feeling like my heart was ripped in half. I was so hurt at the time that I didn't realize that closing off my heart so much would lead me to hurting so many people in the same ways I had been hurt.

I became so good at cutting myself off from feelings and attachment, and when feelings did surface, I was able to cut off the relationship, because I felt on some level like I needed to. That was my mentality. I wasn't vindictive, and I didn't intentionally try to hurt anyone. I just felt a sense of numbness and didn't care. Subconsciously, I thought, *I'm hurt, so why should I care if I hurt you?*

During my late teenage years and early adulthood, I was in so much pain, I had little care for what others were feeling. I missed out on some incredible women and potential partners because of my reckless actions— drinking too much, womanizing, and general disregard for others' feelings as a defense-mechanism to keep myself safe from heartbreak. I was too afraid to lose anyone else, so I would sabotage the relationships.

The biggest thing was that I felt lost, empty, and, other than playing hockey, I lacked purpose and meaning. The only real validation I felt was from the opposite sex, and even that was slowly fading. If girls wanted me or I hooked up with someone, I felt on top of the world. But what I realized was that it faded fast and was just a temporary solution for a deeper problem.

ALCOHOL AND RELATIONSHIPS

Naturally, as young adults, when we become legal age and if alcohol becomes part of our everyday lives, these internal wounds, pain, and trauma can amplify. And if you use alcohol as an escape, things get magnified and come to the surface even more. This is true for everyone, not just young adults. Drinking with intention is important. If you are doing it to celebrate on a special occasion, that's one thing. If you are drinking to numb your social anxiety or fear or deep-rooted pain, these issues you are trying to cover up will only get magnified and will surface in your relationships.

What became evident to me was, once I introduced alcohol into my social interactions with women and in my relationships with them, all my deep-rooted shit started to surface, especially when I overdid it with booze. My behavior when I drank was very different from what I showed on the surface when I was sober. I was always a kind, respectful person and was raised that way. But I had this deep layer of social anxiety and lack of confidence that always brought with it this feeling of doubt. When I drank, I got this boost of confidence, and all that disbelief and lack of confidence went away. And because I loved that feeling so much, I tended to overindulge and end up blacking out.

When I blacked out, I always found out the next day from whomever I was dating at the time that I'd gotten super-angry and said some really nasty things. My partner and I would end up fighting when I was drunk, and I would get super-sensitive, overreact, and say things that were hurtful. I always found I was digging myself out of a hole, and usually what I said wasn't forgivable. This would generally be a turning point in the relationship, because that person was hurt; they took it to heart, and rightfully so.

The problem was that I didn't understand why they couldn't just forgive me. I have realized this is because, when I was growing up, name-calling in my family was the norm. It was all I knew, and it was just part of how I navigated conflict. You get all worked up, say hurtful things, and then just let it bounce off you and forget about it the next day. Unfortunately, it's not that easy with people who haven't grown up with dysfunction in their own lives, and those names are hurtful and stick.

Because I didn't understand their pain, I didn't think too deeply about changing my behavior. This was a pattern that carried on in my life for many years, until I started to address the deep wounds in my subconscious. What was happening is, when I drank, I had no filter, and all that pain, emotion, and sadness I was feeling came to the surface. Having emotional wounds and drinking heavily is like throwing gasoline on a fire. This process took a lot of work, but I got really clear on what these deep wounds were and how alcohol was a catalyst for this behavior.

When I tell my story, people commonly ask me what my turning point was and what made me change my life. That answer is easy. It was December 28, 2017, when I decided to go sober for the entire year and really start to address my problem with alcohol. This was something I had considered many times over, but it was on this day when I reached a breaking point.

I'd gotten tired of feeling like shit and being stuck in this pattern of depending on substances to create my mood. It wasn't alcohol's fault. I knew that not drinking wouldn't "cure" me. However, issues kept surfacing with the opposite sex when I drank, and I couldn't navigate those issues, if I was still drinking. This weird, insecure, jealous feeling always came out, and that would lead to me drinking more, and then all the suppressed feelings of sadness, anxiety, and abandonment would come to the surface.

When I quit drinking for a year, I was in a relationship, and I remember how this commitment to sobriety drastically changed our dynamic. I'd already had those same alcohol-fueled behaviors with her as in other relationships, so she was fully supportive, when I decided to give it up.

This is where things got really interesting. I had a newfound clarity, and I focused on deep personal development work by meditating and, most importantly, gratitude journaling. I also started reading books about people who were having successful lives and who inspired me. I started to really focus on exercise and being mindful of what I put in my body.

This stuff drastically helped me change the deep programming I had in my subconscious, and I found myself not getting angry or saying hurtful things. It was a strange feeling, because it's almost as if in every relationship I was expecting to fuck up somehow and sabotage the whole thing. This time, it wasn't like that. I was able to focus on building on the foundation versus digging myself out of holes.

THE TRANSFORMATION

The healing journey for me and how I relate to a romantic partner has changed dramatically. As I sit here, I realize I have overcome an incredible amount of pain and adversity to get to this point, and I couldn't be more grateful. The main thing is that I have healed a lot of those little-boy wounds that surfaced in my relationships with women. I have had to sit in the discomfort of the pain in order to heal it, rather than escape with alcohol.

Now, if I do drink on occasion, those old wounds and feelings are no longer repressed, so feelings of anger rarely show up. Even on the rare occasions when these feelings have shown up after drinking, whenever I've had a disagreement arise, I no longer lose my shit, say something hurtful, or storm off and cut that person out of my life. Now, I am able to be conscious in the moment and ask myself, *Am I really upset right now? Is this worth even fighting about?* I am able to take a step back and shift my focus to something else, turning an argument into a laugh.

This step is key, and noticing how my reaction changed is when I could tell that I had healed that part of me. My default is no longer anger. I feel a sense of love and compassion and realize that satisfying the drive of my ego to make a point or be right isn't there anymore... Well, at least not enough to go off the deep end with emotion. I have realized that, in moments of conflict, it is important always to remember to come from love and compassion. I am able to catch myself in the moment and ask myself, *What's more important to me—this person I'm with or my stupid drunk opinion?* And the answer is always obvious, when I slow it down and ask.

Relationships will shine a light on our insecurities and weaknesses. They will also bring a lot of loving energy. So, if you can be very honest with yourself, go deep into those dark places, and work on healing them, it will only improve your relationships.

If you think that finding someone will "complete you" or "fill the void" or that you are searching for someone to "make you happy," you will realize that that is just a Band-Aid and all your deep-rooted, unaddressed trauma and issues will surface, even if you're with a wonderful person, and especially if you mix these unaddressed wounds with alcohol. Alcohol itself is not a bad thing, but if it isn't taken seriously, and if you aren't able to manage your emotions with it in a relationship, then it will bring all the shit to the surface in a way that is unproductive. So just be mindful.

"TRAUMA BONDING"—EMBODYING THE VICTIM

Before I started my personal growth and development journey, I found myself embodying the Victim archetype in many areas of my life, particularly my relationships. I believed that I had little control of my life and felt that my partner, or even life in general, was always out to get me when things went wrong. This would lead to me blaming my partner for my emotions, and I would usually throw a pity party that was fueled with rage, fear, anger, and jealousy.

One relationship that stands out to me as a very clear illustration of this was one that I experienced in my late twenties. This was a very intense relationship and I would say the most passionate one I have ever had. It was either super-hot, where we couldn't keep our hands off each other, or it was super-cold, where we were ready to kill each other.

What I realize now, looking back, was that we were both very wounded and had a lot of unhealed trauma that had to be dealt with. And without knowing it, we were trauma bonding. Trauma bonding happens when you feel an attachment to someone who is causing you trauma, pain, or abuse. In this case, we would say very nasty things to each other and then make up. We got into this cycle of yelling and screaming and calling each other names, but then we would make up, showing each other kindness, verbally and through physical affection.

I think because we had both gone through some very challenging moments and pain, we became addicted to the ups and the downs we created. It was a really wild experience, because I did really deeply love her, probably more than anyone I've ever dated, but I was so incredibly insecure about losing her, and I never felt worthy. I constantly lived in this fearful and anxious state, telling myself, *She's going to find some other dude. You aren't good enough for her. You'll lose her and never find someone as beautiful as she is.* So, instead of feeling into that, my Victim self would drink it away, and I would wallow in my own sadness, ruminating on everything that could go wrong, instead of asking myself constructive questions like, "How can I get to the root of this insecurity and codependent feeling?"

From there, I'd go into a sadness, and my insecurities would come out in the form of a pity party. Classic Victim archetype. Often, after our blowout fights, I would continue to indulge in "poor me" thoughts and feelings, instead of examine how I was showing up and contributing to the dysfunction. My insecurity was always steering the ship, and I was addicted to the toxic cycle. The reality of it is I didn't know there was a problem because I actually thought I was in the right and that she was wrong. My level of stubbornness and lack of awareness was classic textbook Victim, and I didn't even realize it.

In this relationship and at this time of my life, I lived in a scarcity mentality, which is a classic tendency of the Victim. I always looked at what was wrong with the relationship versus what was right with it. We both did. It's very common for people to focus on the negative in a relationship versus the positive because of our societal programming, and it really takes effort to practice gratitude in our relationships. I didn't know this at the time, and I never understood the power of focusing on what you *do* have versus what you *don't*. I think this could have really helped in this relationship.

When I look back at this particular relationship, I really can't believe how long we put up with each other. We would get drunk and say the nastiest, most hurtful things, and I think we broke up probably twenty times. But the crazy thing was, when things were good, I never even thought of another person, and I was so attracted to her that those high moments were worth the pain of the low ones.

What I didn't realize at the time, however, was that I wasn't taking responsibility for my actions. I always thought she owed me something or that she would give me the love I didn't feel for myself, but what I realize now is that I was responsible for my happiness; no one else was.

When we can love ourselves deeply, we find another person who aligns with that energy, and you partner up. They aren't completing you like you see in Disney movies. That is a bullshit story made up to make you feel like you are less than, without someone else. Believing that someone else is needed to complete you immediately puts you in this Victim mentality, and you end up attracting other Victims in your life, because you won't take ownership of your own actions and behaviors. What I realize now is that I can cultivate my own love for myself. Then, the boundaries I create for myself honor my truth, and I won't entertain anything that doesn't honor my boundaries. Creating boundaries with yourself and with your partner is super-important, and expressing them is a demonstration of self-love.

Boundary setting is an action of the Warrior archetype—the opposite of the Victim. Warriors fill their own cup, take accountability for their actions, and take complete ownership of their lives... the good, the bad, the ugly.

When I look back at this relationship, I am so grateful because I felt the polarity of hurt and bliss. It showed me what's possible on both sides and gave me a compass to feel into what I actually want.

OWNERSHIP: THE ANTIDOTE FOR THE VICTIM

"Once people stop making excuses, stop blaming others, and take ownership of everything in their lives, they are compelled to take action to solve their problems. They are better leaders, better followers, more dependable and actively contributing team members, and more skilled in aggressively driving toward mission accomplishment. But they're also humble—able to keep their egos from damaging relationships and adversely impacting the mission and the team."

— Jocko Willink

The way to move through the wounded Victim archetype is through ownership. Taking ownership of your life means you are taking complete responsibility for your life and all of your actions and behaviors. This is a key step for moving into the light, into the Warrior energy, but it isn't always easy.

As discussed earlier, living in a Victim mentality means focusing on one's outer world and circumstances. Ownership, on the other hand, is going inward and taking responsibility for one's life or fate.

I speak about gratitude a lot in this book and how it helped me change my focus on all the things I do have versus the things I don't. Gratitude is an essential part of taking ownership.

Your past and your story don't define you, and they shouldn't limit you. Instead, your unique story is what makes you different from everyone else. Your trauma or struggles from the past will become your greatest gifts, if understood, felt, and processed properly. But in order to do this, you must take complete ownership and accountability. You can create new stories if you choose to do so, if you are tired of the old ones running your life. That is a decision that must be made.

You must learn to look at your situation and all of the shit you may have gone through as life lessons and teachers of wisdom. You must realize that every time you fail or get hurt, you build the resilience muscle and get tougher mentally, build more grit, and, most importantly, add another layer to your character. Your mess is your message, and the better you get at owning all the shit in your life and getting excited about it— because no one else has the same stories or knowledge and wisdom you have—the better life gets. This is how you will develop your personal inner strength.

In order to start to take ownership, you must realize every situation and every person you meet is a teacher and a chance for you to grow. Whether an experience is positive or negative, it will serve you in exactly the way that you need it to.

One of the biggest and most important characteristics of being a Warrior and taking complete ownership of your life is the ability to practice empathy and compassion for others. Along with the inability to take ownership, a big part of the population lacks the capacity to show empathy. If you can see the good in people and can remember that everyone is doing their best with what they know and where they're at in their own story and life, it will be easier to have compassion for others.

I know that can be one of the most challenging things to practice, especially if someone has a different opinion or does something that triggers you. This is when it's important to just take a step back and realize that the way they behave has nothing to do with you, and nothing you do can change them. Accepting people where they are at and showing grace is one of the most powerful things you can do.

Often, the harder you are on yourself, the harder you are on others. Once you are able to develop a deeper level of peace within yourself, you will realize that your outer world is a direct reflection of your inner world. The people who take the most radical accountability for their actions and complete ownership don't have time to blame others or expect someone to rescue them, because they are using all their energy to focus on themselves.

If you are truly taking radical responsibility and ownership for yourself and your life, you will notice that you will care less about what others are doing, because they are in control of their lives and their behaviors. This isn't a selfish act; believe it or not, this will actually help all the people around you. All we can do is be kind, do more listening, and open up our hearts a little bit more with compassion and empathy. We must understand that, even if someone angers or triggers us, they were once a young boy or girl, and whether you agree or whether you hate them, nothing you can do will change them. When you find yourself focusing outward, bring it back in and ask yourself, "Am I doing my best and focusing on myself? Or am I focusing on others, waiting for someone to come save me or give me permission?"

When we step out of this wounded Victim archetype and into the empowerment of ownership, we step into healing. The more aware you are and the more you practice, the deeper the level of healing you will experience and the more you will step into the driver's seat of your own life.

As a Warrior, we become witnesses to the inherent emotional master within us all and develop a deep sense of awareness. As said many times in this book, it's not about perfection; it's about identifying when we are playing the Victim by monitoring our behaviors and choosing to step into the antidote of one-hundred-percent ownership.

HEALING THE WAY WE LOVE

When I started to do the healing work on myself, I started to realize that my tolerance for this kind of relationship decreased, and now it is non-existent. I have created non-negotiables for myself and a level of self-love and complete ownership that has allowed me to step out of the blaming and living as a Victim and into the ownership and love of a Warrior.

I've also learned that someone giving you criticism or feedback is always a learning lesson. And if someone is going out of their way to express something to me about my behavior, then I have learned to put my ego aside and listen. Taking a step back, slowing down, and allowing the person to share is so important. Then I'm able to slowly receive the information and actually think about what they are saying. Then, from a place of love and patience, I can speak my opinion.

When you're in the Victim archetype, this isn't possible. Instead of letting the other person finish what they are saying, you interrupt, going on the defensive. You aren't even hearing what they are saying. That will create more resentment between both people, and the other person won't be heard. That kind of behavior will keep you in the backseat of your life, stuck as a Victim.

I'll admit I am still working through this one, specifically with family. I tend to get worked up and react before I let them finish. Taking a deep breath and a step back to let the person speak will save you a ton of unnecessary drama.

My advice to you is to ask yourself: "How am I or how have I shown up as a Victim in my relationships?"

I also want to invite you to really look at your behaviors, and if you find yourself expressing these tendencies in your relationships, maybe you need to figure out why and start getting to the root and healing these parts of yourself before jumping into a new relationship.

Relationships are great, but they will also shine a light on all of your insecurities. They are a mirror looking back at you, so anything you haven't healed in your subconscious, you will most likely attract in another, and it will surface in your life. If you don't have the tools and awareness to deal with it, it won't be pretty. If you have the awareness and can take ownership of your behaviors, then at least you can make the choice to embody the Warrior more frequently.

Healing yourself and those parts are crucial at helping you move out of the Victim archetype and will save you a ton of heartache and pain.

THE FREEDOM OF ACCOUNTABILITY

Part of acceptance is accepting that we cannot control how people feel or how they act or anything happening around us. All we can control is our own energy, the vessel that we have.

We are one-hundred-percent accountable for how we treat our souls and what we allow in them. We are sacred beings, full of potential, and we often do not tap into the truth of who we actually are. We are capable of pretty much anything when we fully put our hearts into it and we believe it, but the problem is there are so many distractions around us. Our reptilian brain's fear and survival response takes over, a carryover from generations of humans having to survive.

When you're in survival mode, you can't create, so the best thing is to get out of our heads and into our hearts. To give ourselves the space to disconnect from the external environment around us, reflect and ask ourselves the question, "What feels true to me?" And when you can find stillness and can ask yourself that question, you can start to get answers that come from your true self, your intuition, rather than the information you get from the people or the news or anything else around you. If we are constantly in fear in survival, we take ourselves out of creation.

MOVING FORWARD THROUGH OWNERSHIP

We've all gone through shit in our lives—we've gone through challenges, we've gone through adversity, we've gone through loss—so until we are super-clear and aware of where we sit and where we stand as a human being with our stories, it's going to be impossible for us to even move forward.

You have to look yourself in the mirror and ask, "Is my life worth it? Is getting out of this mindset of playing a Victim going to bring me where I want to go?"

If you're not willing to be a student of life or willing to be open to opportunities, then you are not willing to change. And you can't make change unless you are open to it. And then, after you are open to change, it's about getting super-radically clear with who you are and then cultivating a deep understanding of why you do the things you do, what those things are, and how you can fix them so that you can move forward.

As we heal and as we grow older, the adversity we face becomes easier; it just becomes part of the game we're in. We aren't broken. We aren't unfixable. What has happened to you is not your fault, but it's up to you to stand in your truth and determine how you are going to change your story. How are you going to change the present-day movie you're running? Are you going to allow the stories of the past to dictate your future? Are you going to keep doing the same things over and over again? Or are you going to take your power back? Can you go stand in truth?

Let's learn about ourselves, learn to love ourselves, learn to love all the shit—the ugly, the good, the bad—because it's part of it. When we can love that within ourselves, then it's easier for us to love and appreciate and accept what comes out of us, out of the people we come in contact with, and out of the world in general. If we are angry and we hate ourselves, and if we hate what we're doing, guess what? We're going to attract more of the same in our life—more of the same people, more of the same shitty experiences—and we're never going to move forward in the right direction.

So just remember, embracing the dark does not mean you become the dark; it means you love the dark, so the dark becomes part of you, because you need the dark as much as you need the light. Otherwise, you become unbalanced. It's all about the polarities in the dualities. You cannot have light without the dark; you can't have dark without the light. When we embrace it, we take our power back, and we enjoy life on a whole new level.

If you don't have accountability for what you can control, then you won't be able to endure adversity. This means, if you aren't accountable for your daily actions and overcoming yourself, then the outside world will always be a lot more challenging. If we can learn to overcome ourselves and our behaviors that keep us playing small, such as not waking up early, being addicted to our phones, eating food that doesn't serve us, or consuming crap on TV, then the external adversity won't be as challenging, because we've conditioned our minds and overcome ourselves.

This is a very important concept to keep in mind, first thing in the morning, because it sets the tone for the entire day. If we know, deep down, that we've done our best, then we don't give a fuck about the outcome, because we put our heart into it. On days when I know I gave everything I've got, I'm unattached to what happens, because I did my best.

On the other hand, there have been days when I have experienced the opposite feeling. In sports, for example, when I knew I didn't give it all I had on the ice or the field, I was left with this feeling of disappointment, this heavy energy of guilt. It's like, "If you know you can do better, then fucking do it."

There are no excuses, but there's also no reason to feel shame. This is a very important part of acceptance and accountability and being able to own your part in order to move through it. We all go through this. Just feel it; understand that you didn't bring it all today. Talk yourself through it. "What did I do well today? What could I have done better? What part of this is mine? Let's bring it tomorrow."

You don't need to get in a shame spiral. This is something that is also characteristic of the Victim archetype. The shame takes you further and further away from being able to do anything about your circumstances. It puts you in a state of lack instead of a state of opportunity. There is no trophy for self-pity. The key is self-reflection on where you could have affected the outcome and how you can do better next time.

Another huge part of accountability is support. Although you cannot blame anyone else for your circumstances, you need to be honest with yourself, if you need help. A helping hand could be necessary if you're battling addiction or truly find yourself in circumstances you can't control. It's moving into the acceptance that you can't do it alone. Maybe you just need help initially to get you into a new situation where you can cope. Enough of this "self-made" shit. This is a Western construct that conditions us into a story to do everything alone. Then when we fail, we go into the shame spiral. It's not meant to be this way. Community is where we thrive and allows us to show up as our best self.

Recognizing where we can do better and where we need help sets us up to win the next time we go through adversity. You can move through it with that same type of grace, which keeps you moving forward. Shame only keeps you in a deep dark hole.

GRATITUDE FOR WHAT IS

Something that will differentiate one person and their ability to move through adversity from those who let it bring them down is their level of gratitude.

When I first heard about the concept of consciously practicing gratitude, I thought it was a silly idea and that its impact would be minimal, but I decided the position I was in currently wasn't a position I wanted to stay in, and I was willing to listen to the people who were having success. So, I picked up the book *The Magic* by Rhonda Byrne.

This book is a twenty-eight-day gratitude practice. ry day, you write down the ten things you're grateful for and why and you really feel them. After reading them over, you say, "Thank you, thank you, thank you."

There's also an exercise to complete each day that allows you to stay in this position of gratitude as much as possible. I have seen a lot of people change from reading and working through this book, and it certainly helped me, so I highly recommend it. Even if it sounds silly to you, like it initially did to me, I invite you to put the judgment aside and try it.

I personally made one tweak to it and now focus on five things I am grateful for and five things I am grateful for that have not yet happened; things that I want to manifest into reality. This is a great exercise for creating the future you want. Try to *really* feel yourself already having that thing and all that comes with it.

Gratitude is more than just saying you're grateful; it's a feeling. The difference between somebody who says they're grateful versus somebody who actually means it is the emotion attached to the words. The better you get at this, the faster things will start to flow into your life.

What I started to notice was the pessimistic attitude that once used to take over my thoughts started to dissipate. I started to notice that I was happier, I looked at life through a better perspective, and I was attracting better opportunities and better people. My life simply improved in just twenty-eight days.

I started to realize how powerful gratitude actually was, and as I started to study more people like Joe Dispenza, to see the science behind the frequency that gratitude holds, I realized gratitude is the ultimate state of receiving. At a vibrational level, it's at one of the highest frequencies, so the longer you can be in that state, the more of that higher vibration at a higher energy you will attract.

One key factor I want to note here is that we are all energy. This is actually proven science and quantum physics. We are all operating at a frequency, and each feeling or emotion has a frequency. The higher the frequency, the better quality the energy. Love, joy, and gratitude are the highest levels of frequency, so when you are able to bring your energy up to those strong frequencies, you become a match to those frequencies you want to attract. The more you can get to or stay in those frequencies or vibrations, the more you become a magnet and a match for those frequencies you want to attract. Like attracts like, and when you are able to change your energy and your state, you will be able to essentially change your life.

Not all of us know or understand how gravity works; we just trust that it does, right? That's kind of the attitude we need to have with gratitude and love in abundance. When we look at life from a perspective of optimism and curiosity versus Victim mentality and fear, life just gets easier, and it gets better. Your quality of life changes, and everything you experience when you look at things from an optimistic, glass-half-full approach just becomes part of it. The powerful lesson I learned from gratitude was that the more you can get to that state and the more you embody that state, the better your life and the better the quality of experiences you'll attract.

Starting your mornings with gratitude programs your subconscious mind and your conscious mind into this state. Sometimes, it takes days, and sometimes, it takes weeks and weeks of programming, but eventually, you can reprogram yourself so that this higher vibration is your default state.

Sometimes, embodying gratitude is as simple as looking at what you have in the world versus what you lack. If you can become conscious of that and you can really look at things with a genuine sense of appreciation instead of a sense of lack, your whole life will change.

This is a process that takes daily work, because it contradicts deep programming. But I promise, if you apply this to your life and you're committed, your life will change and your darkest moments won't be as dark anymore.

CHAPTER 8

STEP #3: ASPIRE

"I firmly believe that, unless one has tasted the bitter pill of failure, one cannot aspire enough for success."

— A. P. J. Abdul Kalam

One of the hardest parts about making change is letting go of a past identity. Depending on how long that identity has been a part of your life and has served you, how much validation you received from that identity, and how much it is ingrained in your psyche, it is going to be a challenge to let it go.

It's important to understand that this isn't about denying this identity; it's about understanding the point at which that identity no longer supports your greater good. You have to identify when that identity is becoming something that is stopping you from really stepping into your greatness, according to your truest self. Your ego gets very attached to the identity it has created, because it has given you validation; it has given you the makeup of who you are and how you see your place as a human being in this world.

You've created your life, or at least part of your life, with this identity, and with identity comes the behaviors and actions that align with it. What becomes challenging is, if you do want to create a new identity, then the actions you must take have to be different, and they must align with a new identity you want to create. We tend to have the habit of doing the same thing over and over again and living our lives in the present moment from stories of the past. What comes before aligning our actions with this true identity is that we must aspire to become them. We must move through life with the belief that we are not only capable of stepping into this higher self but also that we are deserving of it.

All we really know is what happened to us prior to today, the stories we told ourselves, the people we have met, and all of the failures and things we may not yet have accomplished, as well as all the good things we have accomplished. When it comes to understanding your current identity, even if it's something you want to change, it's important to recognize that that identity served you and served a purpose.

Even though you want to change, there are going to be some very positive aspects that you need to be aware of. Changing your identity requires an understanding of why you chose your current one. Do you ever wonder why you decided to pick the character you are? Because that's really what we're doing. We're agreeing to move through life, mostly subconsciously, as the person we were told we needed to be all of those years ago. We are doing all the things that will identify with that character, almost like we are playing in a movie.

Most times, the character, persona, or identity we have chosen isn't who we really are. Usually, we chose something that was constructed by others, by validation, by a social construct, or because it was easier to just commit to being that person rather than someone who may be a little more challenging to be, someone who would be more uncomfortable or outside the box or who may challenge others' identities.

What begins to happen is we have a battle of the identities. If we aren't living in truth and on our intuitional soul path, then we always have this feeling within us that we aren't really doing the thing we really desire. It's a constant tug-of-war between logic and heart, between your mind and your soul.

This is why some people go into depression and have an underlying lack of self-worth or of fulfillment, because they know inside that they aren't living in truth. They aren't living the life they want to live, because they are living someone else's story.

The fact is there are two types of people: those living in their truth and those living someone else's life. The ego will do a great job keeping you safe, but it will also keep you playing in an arena you are used to. If you're used to playing it safe, then the ego will do a good job at keeping you there. And because it gets so much validation from playing that character, the ego will make it very challenging for you to say it's time to play a new character in this world. Your ego is going to want to hold on to your current character, because it feels good, it's easy and familiar, and because the world has rewarded you for it in some way or another. There is always a payoff for staying in this character we're playing.

Unfortunately, the rewards might not be all that rewarding. Your current identity may have roped you into some sort of addiction, whether to fulfill a chemical imbalance, to numb yourself, or to give you dopamine hits. Because of this, people often do not move to change their life. They become addicted to the comfort of knowing what to expect from their behaviors and chosen lifestyle. You've wired your brain to believe this is how life is, and it's challenging to see anything different. Your body strives for homeostasis, and disruption of this is a threat to your existence... or at least the ego believes it is.

There is a time when you just have to get clear and decide change needs to occur. We all know when something isn't serving us, yet we ignore it and then go on autopilot. Sometimes, oftentimes, people will have to face deep pain before they are able to see things clearly and make a change.

The critical piece that allows us to make a change is stepping into gratitude and acceptance of the character we played to release shame and aspire to whoever we are meant to be. Once we come to terms with who we were, we can come to terms with the fact that we've outgrown this character and release them with love.

LANCE, THE SHAPESHIFTER

I experienced three distinct identities: the hockey player, the bartender, and the entrepreneur. These were all different characters I chose to play in the movie of my life. During some of the moments in each of these movies, I did whatever I could to keep that character alive. Aspiring to become our truest self is knowing when it is time to change the costume and move into a new role.

One of the most challenging areas of adversity people face is knowing when it's time for the movie to end. For me, moving out of the hockey player character was very difficult. I was very good at a young age, so my ego was inflated by outside validation growing up. But as my whole world flipped upside down, that's when hockey and my life started to slip. The adversity I faced going through my own personal challenges—living away from family and friends, living with a stepmom with four kids, and getting bullied at my new school in seventh grade—made it really tough for me to keep going. Rather than aspiring to be a better athlete, it took me over, and I looked to unhealthy avenues. It became about trying to escape the feelings of sadness and loneliness rather than making it professionally. I let the adversity take control of me. After my hockey career ended, because of my own lack of commitment and my own mistakes, I was left feeling very empty, because I identified as a hockey player. I didn't know who else to be because my identity was so wrapped up in this hockey character. This is when the real battle between my higher self and my ego began.

I knew it wasn't serving me when I started to drink and party, but it led me to the bar scene, which gave me validation, because I was able to meet interesting people, get attention from women, and be revered as an important person in this world. When I took on the character of the bar manager at the restaurant, I adopted certain behaviors in order to fulfill that character. I was able to drop the hockey player character because I simply replaced one means of validation with another. I didn't aspire to be better; I simply swapped my identity due to my addiction to the outside world's approval.

At the time, it appeared that many positive things were coming out of that lifestyle, making it very hard to change, because that character made me feel like a rockstar. I had freedom to travel, freedom to party, financial freedom, freedom to meet beautiful women, and access to parties and VIPs—it was really amazing. But at the end of the day (or morning, in many cases), it felt extremely empty inside when the lights came on and the hangover subsided. I felt lost and confused and suffered from horrible anxiety.

Despite all of this, I've always known I was destined for greatness. I've always had an internal knowing that there was more for me. I think that's why I allowed myself to try so many things and then leave so many things. A lot of us share this internal knowing, but we choose to ignore it to avoid rocking the boat. We let our egos talk us out of the greatness that we are destined to become. We ignore the whisper and choose instead to listen to our stories and our conditioning. We all have that whisper, and if we don't listen to it, it gets louder and louder. When you keep numbing it with external sources, then you'll eventually be shown it in a much louder way. My whispers turned into yells when I was laying my head down at 6:00 a.m. with heart palpitations and "night" sweats. This was when I quit my job and got out of the industry, forcing myself to start from scratch.

I got tired of feeling unfulfilled; I got tired of feeling tired, beat up, and just deflated. At the end of the day, when I knew I needed to change course in my path, I had to ask myself, "Does this character still serve me? Or is it hurting me? Does this person align with the person I desire to be?"

I knew the answer was sobriety, but alcohol was something deeply ingrained into my lifestyle, because I was working in it. It was the most challenging thing to beat. When I decided to take a year off drinking, my entire life changed. When I drank, I not only slept terribly, but I also ate badly, and I had a complete lack of motivation for anything else, especially learning, growing, and working on myself. So, when I decided to quit drinking for one year, my life got a lot less cloudy. My body wasn't having to constantly repair itself from the toxins in my system. I ate less junk food, I slept better, I slimmed down, and I was in amazing shape.

These were the things I had to do in order to become the person I wanted to be. After a while, I realized I no longer wanted to work in the bar, restaurant, and hotel environment. It just didn't serve me, because I had been unplugged from the world of alcohol for so long, it didn't feel in alignment with who I was becoming. I was spending my evenings serving people something that I didn't value in my own life anymore. That, in combination with the healthy behaviors I adopted and the personal-development work I was doing, led me to make another career change. Slowly, I started to uncover the fact that I needed to do something of meaning; I needed to do something that could impact people. Eventually, I asked myself, how can I make the biggest impact with my story? That eventually led to the birth of *University of Adversity.*

Part of learning how to master adversity is looking to others who have mastered it themselves. It's about gaining new information, knowledge, hacks—whatever you want to call it—so you can move through it yourself and, ultimately, use adversity to your advantage.

In early 2018, I read the book *Crushing It* by Gary Vaynerchuk, in which he exposes all of his entrepreneurial strategies for growing his companies and creating massive wealth. The one thing that really stood out to me was the importance of starting a podcast. I had learned so much from listening to Joe Rogan's podcast for years, as well as to so many others, such as Tim Ferris, Aubrey Marcus, Dave Asprey, Lewis Howes, Tom Bilyeu... the list goes on.

As a listener, there was a certain amount of trust I had in people who were able to speak their truth without having an agenda. In this environment and in this format, no one was telling them what to say; they could just be real. I loved the raw, honest dialogue and couldn't get enough of it. I realized that so many of the guests on the shows I was tuning into shared stories of painful times and how they rose above it to become a huge success. Over and over again, I'd hear these stories. After a certain point, I realized it was my calling. I, too, had experienced many levels of adversity and somehow overcome it. I lived to tell the tale, and I wanted to help others by bringing them those same stories of adversity. And not just the sexy story of success, but the harrowing journey that often led up to that point. So, at the very end of December 2018, I started the *University of Adversity* podcast.

My mission for the show was to feature powerful guests who provide tools, tips, resources, and hacks gained from their experience with adversity in order to allow others to shorten the learning curve from struggle to breakthrough. Ultimately, I really wanted to open up the doors to powerful stories and share those stories, allowing listeners to gain a better understanding of themselves.

After realizing the value of my own podcast, I started a media company, Mic-Up Podcast Productions, as I was passionate about helping other business owners and entrepreneurs acquire the same tool I had. My vision was to give people this personal brand accelerator and have all the work done for them, so they could just show up on the court and make the baskets. I saw what this powerful tool was doing in my own life, so I felt I needed to provide the same thing to others.

While this journey has been extremely rewarding, in true brand fashion, I will share that it hasn't been a walk in the park. This journey in itself has been one of the most challenging I've had in the last two years. I've had to deal with unhappy clients. I've had to deal with partnerships that have gone sour, rebranding several times, thousands of dollars lost in poor business decisions, hiring the wrong people—all the things that can happen have happened. This entrepreneurial journey has taken a flashlight and shined it on every single weakness and aspect of my life. Having a podcast and a podcast agency has been really challenging because of the competitive nature of the market as well as the constant comparison and challenges that come with a growing and changing industry.

I am so grateful for the ups and downs, though, because, if you don't become aware of your weaknesses, you will never know what they are, and you will never be able to change them. The podcast has given me the opportunity to expand on so many things that wouldn't otherwise have been possible. This journey has been humbling and has transformed me into a student of life. The more I learn, the more I realize I don't know shit! Well, that's not true. I know some things. Either way, in the end, it makes me happy to know that, as I grow and learn more skills as an entrepreneur, they allow me to have more empathy and respect for where other people are at.

As I sit here today, writing this book, I can honestly say I'm at a level of wholeness I have never been before. That has come from many hours of my commitment to change and from aspiring to be my very best, through many years of failures, of course. It's not easy to become a new character in the world we live in, but if you were hired to star in a movie, wouldn't you at least aspire to demonstrate the actions and behaviors of that character?

What must come before this is structuring one's life in a way that supports this new character. In the real world, you can't aspire to lose twenty pounds when you're surrounding yourself with junk food. You can't aspire to be healthy and sober when you're surrounding yourself with the bar scene and drunk idiots. You can't aspire to be a massive success when you're surrounding yourself with people in a scarcity mindset with no motivation.

THE LAW OF ATTRACTION

This is a very powerful tool, if you understand it and use it correctly. The Law of Attraction isn't about wishing for a new car and then a car just appears. There's a lot more to it. Not only is the Law of Attraction about visualizing what you desire, what you want to bring into your life, but what's just as important, if not more important, is truly embodying what it would feel like to have that thing in your presence now.

So, as Dr. Joe Dispenza talks about, what you want to do is have a clear intention and an elevated emotion. If you can get good at being able to cultivate that, you will be able to bring what you desire into your life faster and easier.

But that's only one part of it. There's also part of it where you need to take action; there's a certain amount of work that needs to be done in this reality. Your actions and behaviors have to align with the person you desire to be or the person who has the things you want to attract into your life. So, if you are able to visualize and you are able to get to the feeling, really embracing and embodying what it feels like to have that thing, when you can see who you are with and what the weather is like outside, what it smells like to completely embody the feeling of having the thing or desire that you want, when you're as clear as you can possibly be in your vision and the feeling and then take those inspired actions you need to take in the present moment in order to get that thing, *then* it will happen.

A lot of people miss these final steps. Again, your actions have to be aligned with the actions it takes to get the thing that you want. All you can do is simply the best that you can in the present moment, so you want to be at the highest level of vibration, the highest frequency you possibly can be. When you're at that high level of frequency, you're able to attract more of that into your life. When you're feeling like that, and you take that inspired action and take the first step and then the next step then all the subsequent steps, the things you need or the people you need to meet will appear in your life. And then the path will open up for you. That's how the Law of Attraction works—for better or for worse, it will give you more of what you put out into the Universe.

In my own life, I started to just visualize the things I wanted to create for myself. I wanted to embody and be *that* person. I started to map out an exercise called the Perfect Day, where you envision your future self in an environment where you've accomplished all that you've wanted to accomplish. You envision who you're with and the place you want to be. This was a powerful exercise for me, and in order for me to start to make changes in my life, I needed to take the actions this person would take.

I visualized, practiced gratitude, and connected to my higher self or soul. When you meditate, you're able to quiet down the external noise in order to see what is true, which is your heart and your soul.

There was always this lingering feeling within me that I knew I could be doing better and I could be doing more, but there was this resistance in my way that wouldn't allow me to take action. The powerful thing about doing these kinds of exercises is that it rarely shows up as you expect. That's the big part people miss, when they try to control the outcome of it. When we fixate on the outcome, we risk missing out on the beautiful opportunities that present themselves. It's important to be flexible and without judgment.

Sometimes, what we call in and attract into our lives is going to be adversity, and sometimes it's going to be a challenge, but in order for us to get the level we're aspiring to, we have to overcome that. The Law of Attraction can bring more adversity into our lives that will serve us long term. I could never have imagined how my life was going to unfold when I did this work, but I just continued to commit myself to growth and doing what I could to heal the things that were holding me back and getting in the way of me seeing life clearly.

Once you start to get to a certain level of wholeness when working on yourself, you realize you don't need as much, because you feel fulfilled. Then, guess what? When you feel whole and fulfilled, you start to attract more abundance into your life. That's where I am now. In the past, the more I gripped onto things and the more tense I got, the more I closed myself off. The more I realized how I did my best in those moments when I let go of the outcomes, the more things were able to just flow in. It's been a really interesting dance in my life to see how it's all flowed.

Has it all worked out? No, but I don't have the end result of what that's going to look like, so possibly all of this stuff I've gone through was all part of it, so I can eventually reach my highest potential. This perspective wouldn't be possible without an understanding of The Law of Attraction.

Tune into Episode #195 on *University of Adversity* with Jack Canfield, America's leading authority on success and personal fulfillment and bestselling co-author of the *Chicken Soup for the Soul* series. Canfield is also one of the amazing stars in the movie, *The*

Secret, in which he explains the Law of Attraction in great detail.

IMPOSTER SYNDROME

In my opinion, "imposter syndrome" is not a phrase that serves people. People have gotten hung up on this feeling. The reality is, there's nothing wrong with feeling like an imposter, because if you want to improve yourself and evolve into a higher version of you, there is going to be a level of discomfort. You're going to feel like you're being somebody else, because the person you're aspiring to be is going to feel unfamiliar. You're engaging in behaviors you may never have engaged in before, or maybe not consistently. You are going to feel like you're impersonating someone else because, essentially, you are. You are doing the things to rise to the identity of that new human you desire to become.

Connecting with your potential and the highest version of yourself is not an easy thing to do. When we want to aspire to move forward in our lives and move into a new energy and a new environment, there's going to be a certain amount of resistance that comes. This is to be expected.

A large part of the adversity we face is our own selves. We will face external adversity many times in our lives, but the biggest adversity you'll face is overcoming yourself each day. If you are willing to change your behavior on a daily basis to aspire to be the person you hope to become, then you will absolutely get there.

The biggest way to combat "imposter syndrome" is to continuously identify the behaviors of the highest version of you, and then practice them, day in and day out. The first time I learned about this, which really flipped the concept of "imposter syndrome" upside down, I was listening to Seth Godin on Aubrey Marcus's podcast. This was the first time that I had ever heard somebody talk about imposter syndrome this way, and it really helped me understand that this word can be so limiting in that we use this word almost like an easy way out.

There were so many times on my own journey when I felt unworthy of praise, unworthy of the things that had been brought into my life, the people had attracted, or the experiences and opportunities I was presented with, and this was because I was so attached to a past story that I didn't feel I was worthy to create a new one. I felt like a fraud. That's where a lot of the work starts— the understanding that your past does not define you; it is not your identity.

In order to really become the person you want to be, you have to think about what this person actually looks like. Visualize this day in and day out. This is where I truly believe people who visualize more, people who meditate about creating their future self, people who journal and get really clear about what that person looks like so they can feel it in their bones each day, will experience a lot less imposter syndrome because they've already conditioned their mind to believe that they *are* that person. Of course, if you're not familiar with what that person looks like or feels like or the actions that person would take, it's going to feel foreign and you're going to feel like a phony. But the more you imagine this as your current reality, the deeper you get into becoming that person before it happens, then the less difficult it's going to be when you're living your daily life in this 3-D reality.

A critical piece of being able to move through this part of the journey of adversity is releasing shame around any unpleasant feelings that come up along the way. Understand that these feelings are normal. I've also realized that we tend to think that a lot of other people have it all figured out already, and we're alone in what we're feeling. What I've been blessed enough to discover from interviewing very successful people who have achieved a lot in their lives is that they're all human, too, and have gone through all of these same feelings of being an imposter.

Identity work is vast and deep when we are reaching for that next level. We like to look at successful people as though they've discovered the secret code to life. While most of them have discovered a pathway to success, it was discovered through a fuck-ton of pain, discomfort, and uncertainty. Everyone's path and circumstances are different, and we can't look at one's journey through a cookie-cutter lens.

An important key to being able to step into this role of who you aspire to be is developing confidence. But confidence doesn't just come out of the sky; confidence is built through daily practice. I have tested this on myself many times. When I stick to my morning routine, when I get up at the time I say I'm gonna get up, when I make my bed, when I do my meditation, when I do my journaling, when I do some reading, all before I turn on my phone, I just feel better. It's like the Universe and God are giving me a pat on the back and high-five, saying, "Good job! You did it! Way to go!" And then I feel accomplished, first thing in the morning.

The small wins are what build confidence, and as we move throughout our day and into our craft or our business, they are a key element in aspiring to our greatest self. We need to stand tall in this person consistently, every single day, if we want to become that person.

Throughout my journey of personal development, I've tried so many different routines, and I've kind of developed my own mix of all of them, because I have become conscious of what works best for me personally. I've discovered that, for me, the simplest things are the best. The most important thing is getting up when I say I'm going to get up, and usually my best time to get up is between 4:30 a.m. and 5:30 a.m. This is challenging for me to stick to, but when I do get up and I do condition my body to maintain that routine, it allows me to build the level of confidence needed to keep evolving into the best and most capable version of me.

The reason many people aren't able to get to this point is that they aren't able to cultivate the necessary awareness or acceptance of their past in order to move into the space of stepping into the belief they can achieve what they want or become who they want to be. They allow their story of the past to take hold of them and waste away in the comfort of knowing what to expect, even if it isn't truly what they want. But comfort is not the thing that is going to help you use adversity to your advantage to create a life worth living.

The person you aspire to be needs to be at the forefront of your life and your mind each and every day. How does this person act? How do they walk? How do they talk? How does their mind work? Who do they surround themselves with? What have they accomplished? Visualize this as clearly and specifically as possible, write it down, put it in a place you see every day, and read it over and over again until it becomes your reality.

This is why people who are actors rehearse and go over the script and read over their lines and eat, sleep, and breathe their roles. They go over it all, day in and day out, until they become that character. It's the same in real life. The more you rehearse, the more you embody that character you want to evolve to, and the easier it's going to be, and the less you will feel this so-called "imposter syndrome."

When I first started my podcast, I experienced so many moments when I questioned if I was worthy to interview a famous guest. And each time was an opportunity to step deeper into my highest identity and dive into this belief by continuously visualizing myself crushing each interview. Because of my ability to make this belief a part of my identity, I've interviewed hundreds of amazing people.

When I first started as a podcast host, I didn't really have much to lose. I just felt lucky to be able to have anyone on the show who would come on. I would get sent guests and would just be happy to be doing it, happy to be interviewing anybody. What was really interesting was that I was getting sent *great* people, and as I started to interview more and more, I started to realize that this was something I was meant to do.

I used a certain tactic, something I realized I had picked up from my many years in the bar industry. I was able to connect with people and break down the barriers to get them to open up and really have a heartfelt conversation. I was able to do that in the bar industry; I was able to learn people's stories without even realizing I was doing it. It was just something I generally enjoyed doing. I loved learning about people and asking questions and seeing them open up. A level of trust would open up in these conversations, where things would just flow and connect and then great energy and great ideas would arise.

I realized I could be great at this skill. It really wasn't anything but just being myself and being the curious person I am. When I have conversations and interview people, I come at it with genuine curiosity about them. I take a general interest in who they are. And so, as I started to become more confident, I started to get better at my delivery. I started to get better at asking interesting questions, and I started to develop way more confidence in a belief that I belonged there with these other people.

But that didn't come easily, because as I started to become more experienced, I also put more pressure on myself to be at a certain level, to hit certain numbers— all of the vanity metrics you hear about in the podcast world. I started to compare myself to others. I started to doubt myself at times. So then, when I had a big guest, sometimes I would hope that they would cancel, because I was so nervous.

There were days when I didn't feel worthy to have certain people on my show. What I had to do was dig deep and look at what that really was about. I had to ask myself, "Why do you believe you are incapable of doing this?" When I looked at myself in the mirror, I couldn't find a good answer.

When I look back at my life experiences, through hockey to too many years in the bar and restaurant industry, I can see that I am a very well-rounded, versatile human and I can connect with just about anybody. Even though I wasn't at the same success level as some of the people I was interviewing, I still had a ton of value to bring to the conversation and to their life, because I'm a powerful force of energy. I knew that my worth was only going to come from the belief I had in myself, so if I projected that I wasn't confident and didn't believe in myself, that's what these people were going to see. I really got clear with myself to understand that I did have a seat at the table with any of these people, because I was going to be successful. I had to put myself in a frame of mind where I already had that success and had a show of the magnitude I desired.

When I interviewed people like Grant Cardone, Dean Graziosi, Jack Canfield, and other very successful people, I had to get in the mindset that I belonged there. I had to do what I had to do to get to that level, and that process itself, knowing I had to bring my A-game in preparation, in energy, in all of the things to get to that level of confidence and belief, to be able to know that I belonged there, was such a powerful lesson in itself.

So, as you can imagine, when you start to have these high-level conversations consistently, about three interviews a week, you become that high-level interviewer yourself. You become that person, because your energy and your vibration is at the level of this elevated conversation more often than not. When you're speaking to people at that level, you ascend to that level.

After a while, I noticed that my confidence skyrocketed. Being able to tap in and have a real conversation, to have these people open up and tell me how they'd never talked about certain things to anyone before me and then for me to share my part of the story, has helped me grow beyond comprehension. Being able to bounce ideas and stories off these successful people and have them really listen has been one of the most powerful things I've ever experienced.

I have gotten messages from listeners about how these episodes changed their lives, or how they got something out of the episode that helped them make a difference. And that's really what it's all about, as are the relationships I've been able to build throughout this podcast.

There is no doubt that my communication skills and my belief in myself are at a completely different level than they were only three years ago. I have been able to change my life and do all the things I'm doing now because I set up the foundation with this podcast.

I knew I had to do it, and sometimes when you do things that you know you have to do, they just line up. I've been so blessed because my own career has literally been the number-one personal-development tool for me; it's literally been therapy for me. Now, I'm able to tap into something I always knew was possible. As I continue to grow, I continue to discover new levels of my potential, and I continue being able to harness my true voice to share stories of truth, resilience, and overcoming adversity.

This unwavering belief in yourself, however, doesn't come overnight; it comes from small wins along the way that you become brave enough to expose yourself to. It comes from stepping into and owning your power and from really understanding that you are in this position for a reason; you are on a fucking mission.

You deserve to be exactly where you are. You don't owe anybody anything. The only person you owe anything to is to yourself, to keep those commitments and the promises with yourself that continue to build that confidence, which only instills a greater level of belief.

So, get used to those uncomfortable moments and get used to owning it, realizing that nobody has all of their shit figured out. They are all just scared little kids who decided they were worthy of more. Remember: no matter the success somebody has or the status they've achieved, we are all just human beings, and everyone was in the same position you are, at one point or another. Instead of saying "imposter syndrome," think of it as "future self-embodiment." Who do you want to be, and how are you going to embody that today?

WHAT I LEARNED AFTER SPENDING SEVEN DAYS WITH DR. JOE

In August 2021, I was blessed to spend a total of seventy-two hours in the direct presence of the incredible Dr. Joe Dispenza for the first time. This man forever changed how I look at my ability to heal myself.

Joe Dispenza is somebody I discovered around the same time I really got serious about my journey of transformation. I heard about him for the first time back in the mid-2000s, in the movie *What the Bleep Do We Know?* However, he wasn't on my radar until about 2017, when I really started to do the personal development work. At the same time, I discovered gratitude practice, meditation, and the Law of Attraction.

A lot of personal-development concepts were difficult for me to grasp, because I didn't understand the science behind them. What I really appreciated about Dr. Joe Dispenza was his ability to combine the mystical with science in an easily digestible way. So, while I was learning and applying practices like gratitude and meditation, I was able to learn the science behind why it actually worked. That is the reason most people are skeptical about the stuff. They want to know the science. Dr. Dispenza backs up so much of what he does with science, studies, and data.

I then read his book *Becoming Supernatural*, which I highly recommend, and I listened to him on many podcasts, including Aubrey Marcus and Lewis Howes—pretty much all of the big podcasts have had him on at some point. I plan on getting him on my show, too.

I really didn't understand the magnitude of his work until I saw what went on at his retreats. In my opinion, he's doing some of the most important work on this planet. Dr. Dispenza is giving people the tools they need to be able to heal themselves. He is empowering people to look inside and see how they already have everything it takes. And while he's doing this, he is giving people the tools to be able to help heal others—just by opening and tapping into their hearts and having the brain and heart work together, connecting the divine and unlimited potential.

The opportunity presented itself to go on a week-long intensive retreat, and I quickly jumped on it. His events sell out very quickly, and I was blessed to be able to get a ticket to his event in Denver, Colorado, in 2021.

The retreat was indescribable. The schedule consisted of meditations that started between 4:00 a.m. and 6:00 a.m., then we had a late-morning walking meditation. We finished off the day with heart coherence healing, where we would actually do meditations to heal volunteers. Throughout the day, we had breaks, meals, and more meditation. We learned about scientific studies on spiritual concepts and listened to doctors lecture about these topics.

It was really profound. If there was any shred of doubt about this work, it was eliminated when I witnessed the healing take place. I saw people get up out of their wheelchairs and walkers for the first time.

After doing the meditations, I opened up my heart to a level I never thought possible, and that is exactly what I needed to see and feel in order to understand the human potential we are capable of. So, when I talk about this stuff, it's not just spewing out bullshit. This stuff is real, and I want people to realize how powerful we are, if we fully believe, if we fully commit to healing and empowering ourselves by tapping into our unlimited potential.

Feeling fulfilled in everything life has to offer us is the secret sauce to alchemizing our adversity into rewards. And it's such a beautiful thing to know that, within us, we have access to everything we need to cultivate the energy, to be able to see ourselves, and to completely change our lives. Dr. Dispenza says, when you change your energy, you change your life, and I believe it. I felt it, I saw it, and my life will never be the same.

Dr. Dispenza moves you into a higher plane with his high-vibration influence of happiness, joy, and love—the vibration of abundance. If you want to attract abundance in your life, and it's not just money, but wealth in all areas, essentially, you're seeking freedom and you're seeking wholeness, joy, and love. It was beautiful because he told us a lot of people come to his events seeking something external and then, through his guidance, discover that what they seek is actually love for themselves and inner wellness/wholeness.

He taught us the importance of opening our hearts and keeping them open because, in our world, in our society, it's so easy for us to close our hearts and shut down permanently. He explains that, if you're able to keep your heart open each day and tap into the energy of joy and love early in the morning, you're more able to keep that throughout the day and, therefore, more able to rise above the bullshit. You then position yourself to tap into your divine unlimited potential.

Each day for seven days, I got up between 3:00 and 4:30 a.m. to meet for the daily seminars between 4:00 a.m. and 6:00 a.m. Before we went into the retreat, we didn't know the daily schedule at all; we just had to show up.

This is when Dr. Joe began to dial in the psychology behind the entire week. He didn't want it to be predictable for anyone or allow the attendees to create stories around what their experience would be like. Genius, if you ask me. And quite frankly, I'm glad he did this, because I was in no way prepared for what was about to ensue. Little did we know, on Day 6, we were going to do a four-hour pineal-gland meditation. Being that we only learned of this after it was finished, it forced us to adapt to the present moment.

The pineal gland, also known as the third eye, is located in the middle of your head, toward the back. It's important to have a healthy pineal gland, which aids in developing a deep spiritual practice. It's the doorway that connects us to time, space, and the supernatural world. The pineal gland also produces melatonin, which is in charge of regulating our circadian rhythm for sleep, and it produces DMT, something you may have heard of in reference to the psychedelic community.

DMT produces a hallucinogenic effect. This can be achieved through your pineal gland via deep meditation and deep breathwork practices. That's why it's so important to have a clear pineal gland, so you can access this world when you are doing meditation and breathwork practice. You want to be able to tap into that radio receiver that opens up the doorway to different dimensions and frequencies.

That's why, over the years, you may have heard of certain things, such as fluoride, among other factors, contributing to calcification of the pineal gland. The implications of this are reduction in sleep quality, and many believe it dampens a deeper connection to ourselves and our spiritual connection to a greater force—or a deeper connection to our innate wisdom, or intuition, which gives us insight and hunches. Calcification of the pineal gland dampens the feeling of purpose in our lives, which could feel like a dullness and lack of a clear channel, like watching an old, low-definition TV versus a new high-definition TV. You can watch the low-definition TV, and you will get used to it, but you can feel the difference when one TV is very clear versus very dull. This is what makes the pineal gland so powerful. It works like a radio receiver: the clearer it is, the clearer the signal you can send out, and the clearer information you receive.

Paying attention and understanding the magnitude and the power of this part of the brain is really important. There are plenty of resources on this topic, and I'm just new to exploring and understanding it myself through Dr. Dispenza's work and through holotropic breathing.

The four-hour meditation was one of the most challenging and irritating experiences I have ever had. Talk about adversity in action. I know that sounds dramatic, but really, picture four hours of sitting with yourself, not able to do anything but stay in the moment without any distractions. Yes, pure torture. At least that's what I felt initially. I was not prepared for this. I didn't bring a blanket or a pillow. I ate too much food the night before. I was in no way ready for this moment, but I did it anyway.

I was so uncomfortable right off the bat because I anticipated it being long and drawn out and miserable. I was tired. I wanted to fall asleep. I wanted coffee. I was cold. My back started to hurt. All these things surfaced.

But the beauty of this was learning to become aware of what I was experiencing, to accept it and breathe through each thought without labeling it. Letting each thought and complaint come and go, come and go, come and go... knowing I would eventually get through it and get to the end. It was a deep metaphor for every shitty time I'd experienced in my life. None of those broke me, and neither would this. And I would come out stronger than I was before, just like all those other times. Eventually, that pain and discomfort have to transmute into a feeling of love, once you move through it.

There were certain meditations during the week where it actually felt like I was going to burst into tears because of how challenging it got. We would sit in a chair up to ninety minutes, and sometimes, it felt like my legs were on fire. My hips were so sore, eventually going numb. Every sensation in my body became heightened, and right at that moment when I felt ready to give up, Dr. Joe said, "All right, without breaking your state, lie down."

Another metaphor for adversity. Just when you think you can't handle it anymore, just when you think you have nothing left, you hang on just for one more moment... and it's over. You've done it. Then, the tears came, but instead, these were tears of gratitude and pride for making it this far.

Quieting my mind is exactly the medicine I needed for my life, and this experience began to really nurture that within me. The biggest challenge for me in that moment—and in life—is just letting go and trusting. If you can overcome yourself, you can overcome anything. And isn't that really what our journey is? It's not the people who are telling us, "You can't do it." It's overcoming ourselves every single day. We're the biggest barrier. It's stepping into the belief of what we're capable of and curating our environments to reflect that belief. I chose to be in this room with hundreds of powerful people because I knew I belonged there. And to be in that collective energy of people who had that belief even before starting only amplified the massive transformations everyone was having.

This part of the journey is so critical because, without the belief in all that we're capable of, we will continue to look at adversity through the lens of a victim. We will continue to stay attached to a story that we are broken, that we need fixing, that we aren't worthy of everything we desire. And we will create our world to match that belief.

The danger of this is that all of our thoughts, emotions, and language hold a vibrational frequency. If you're going to play in this low-level vibrational frequency of doubt, fear, ego, and victimhood, then you're essentially setting yourself up to attract that same kind of bullshit. It's important to understand that change takes work. It takes commitment. It takes discipline. It takes being willing to experience short-term discomfort (like a four-hour meditation) for long-term happiness.

CHAPTER 9

STEP #4: ALIGNMENT

"A lot of the conflict you have in your life exists simply because you're not living in alignment; you're not being true to yourself."
— Steve Maraboli

We live in a society that is based on consumption and consumerism. From a young age, we are conditioned to believe we need something outside of ourselves to fix us or make us whole. We are programmed to think we need the next new thing, like the newest iPhone, or the next magic pill to take all our pain away or lose weight or some person we are dating or some guru to fix us, because we are broken and do not have what others have. We give our power away because we lack trust in ourselves and our own abilities. The reality of it is we have everything we need to be whole already. And unfortunately, the more we feel a lack, the more we feed the need to seek something outside of ourselves in one of the many forms.

We also see this in personal development at times. Don't get me wrong: I am a big fan of personal development, and I owe so much of my healing to it, but I also know there is a certain aspect of it that is meant to make you feel like you still need to keep seeking more information or you won't have all the right answers until you go to the latest seminar. Personal development and books are so important, but people can also fall into this place where they feel like they always need fixing and never quite have enough information.

All of this information we have in the world is such a blessing, but if we don't take the time to apply what we have learned, then we will constantly seek new information, and oftentimes, it is conflicting, which leads to confusion.

So, let's be clear. I am not saying stop doing personal development work or reading or seeking out new opinions and insights. What I'm saying is develop awareness in yourself. If you have done a lot of work, read a lot of books, and you still feel stuck, just reflect on it and ask: Have I actually applied this yet? You might be further along than you think.

WHAT REALLY MATTERS

Personally, I spent a lot of time in the Fixer archetype, constantly feeling broken and like all the answers were outside of myself. After I found personal development, it was like another drug—something that would give me all the answers. It got to a point where I expected it to do all the work for me, losing trust in myself. I finally realized that this tool was simply that: a tool. It was meant to guide me to myself, but I was relying on it to tell me who I was.

I still bounce in and out of this type of self-work, but what has changed over the years is the awareness of when I'm falling into the trap of the Fixer. I have been known to doubt myself a lot, and I can be indecisive at times. This comes from a lack of confidence in what I'm doing and whether what I'm saying will actually be received. Since the beginning of my personal-growth journey, I have improved dramatically in this area, but I'm still not perfect, and you know what? I never will be. And that's okay.

One pattern I fell into was questioning whether the knowledge I had about something I had been learning about was enough to speak on it. I found myself consuming podcast after podcast, book after book, seminar after seminar, until I finally realized... *Wait a minute! I've come a long way, and I may actually know something!* I may come across like I have everything together now, but self-doubt took over my life for many years, and I always found myself seeking permission or approval for what I already knew. I would assume the other person was always right or that my partner would fill the void I had from my own lack of self-love.

I also fell down the spiral of buying lots of nice things, spending lots of money on fancy restaurants, and even though those were fun times, it still always left me feeling empty. It was the same pattern when it came to women. It was the thrill of the chase, and then, after the pursuit was over, it didn't fill the void as I thought it would. I kept seeking these external things to make me feel whole and lacked the characteristics of the healthy masculine—traits like decisiveness and confidence.

I discovered that these traits are built through the simple things, the building blocks, like a morning routine, and that a deficiency in these healthy masculine traits comes from a lack of consistency. Building a solid foundation will compound, over time, into solid confidence, fulfillment, and wholeness. Meditation, journaling, and having a gratitude practice completely changed my entire mindset and rewired my brain to see life differently.

Also, when I started to focus on what I could control versus what I couldn't and took complete ownership of my life, I needed less from the external world, because I created wholeness within. The fact is I was just plain lazy.

There are still days when I think I need to seek more answers as to why I can't maintain self-discipline, or times when I don't feel as whole. This is when I have to own up to my own bullshit and that I am choosing not to do what I know works.

If we learn what works for us and we don't do it, then we will always have an unpleasant sense in the backs of our minds that something isn't right. This is because, when you discover that deep feeling of wholeness, bliss, and confidence, your body loves it. So, if you don't get to that level because of your own actions—choosing something for the sake of ease or something that's out of alignment—that's when those feelings set in. It's not about shaming yourself; it's about taking complete ownership and realizing no one can fix you. You must do the work on yourself and apply it. It isn't always easy, but when you do, your life will change and you will start to embody the Warrior spirit—what it truly means to you—and you will know it!

Something interesting I have observed over years, while traveling and living in different parts of the world such as Mexico, Costa Rica, Thailand, and Indonesia, is that some of the people I met seemed very happy, even though they had very few material possessions. When I landed in Bali, Indonesia, I saw a lot of very small homes, each with many family members in them, shack-like structures covered by tarps. I noticed how simple and basic these homes were, including only the bare essentials. You could see right through the houses; they didn't have walls.

I immediately wondered, *How are people able to live like this?* I couldn't help but feel sorry for them as I walked by. But, over time, as I walked by these houses a number of times, I began to notice the kids playing, the parents and family sitting out front together laughing, and people just enjoying life exactly as it was.

At first, I questioned, *Why aren't these people sad and depressed? Am I missing something here?* Then it dawned on me that maybe having a bunch of possessions or nice things or a nice home doesn't necessarily make you happy. I started to think that maybe all of the stuff we have and all of our technological advancement distracts us from what matters. In other, less-developed countries I've visited, I noticed they seem to value their social time and leisure time. They value the importance of having meals together, community, and fun.

In the Western world, we can get very lost in the pursuit of new things, in getting to the next level and having more. We forget how the things that really matter are right in front of us. And those things are usually what money can't buy: laughter, play, and getting together with friends and family.

It was an interesting thing to reflect on. *If these people who barely have anything to their name are able to smile and enjoy life, could it be that the possessions we seek don't actually bring us the happiness we think they will?*

This is when I started to realize that, in my own life, my happiness comes from making a difference in the world and overcoming the things I thought I couldn't, in order to get to a better place. That is what brings me fulfillment. I've tried buying all the fancy shit many times over, and I've been left feeling, *Is this it?*

Having fancy things is great, don't get me wrong, but having these things once you have realized that these things aren't going to fill a void is a lot different than thinking these things you buy will magically make you happy. It just doesn't work that way. It may work for the short term, but you will always want more. If you don't find fulfillment in yourself first, that chase will never end.

Having the idea in your mind that more is always better will take you out of the present moment and out of gratitude. Presence is key, and giving your full attention to the present moment, the people and whatever it is you are doing, will allow you to value the object, person, or event you are experiencing. When you are fully present, you're not allowing any beliefs from the past or thoughts of the future to give meaning to something. You are just experiencing it for what it is.

When we aren't present, we feel lack and that something is missing. That's when we have thoughts like the future will be better, or we believe, when we meet that one person, we will be complete. The truth is this: the person you desire to be is already here, right now, in the present moment. And if your actions are aligned with that person whom you think about and desire to be and when you embrace elevated emotions with an open heart, you will become that person.

There is never a perfect time. The perfect time is always now.

SELF-CARE

If you are feeling a sense of lack, a sense that you need to be fixed, ask yourself why that is. I bet you nine times out of ten it's because you lack a self-care practice in your life.

Self-care isn't weakness; self-care is actually the strength of a Warrior because Warriors know, if they take self-care seriously, they can perform better. When you practice self-care, your cup will overflow with all the things you may feel you are lacking, like confidence, belief, and general self-love.

General self-love means loving yourself where you are and not boxing yourself into an idea of where you should be—somewhere further ahead than where you are now. This thinking is useless. Self-love means loving all parts of yourself—the good, the bad, the ugly. When you can accept who you are fully, you will start to love who you are, and, in turn, you will love others around you more. You will feel the need to seek less, because you already have everything you need.

Meditation, having a gratitude practice, journaling, and breathwork are the biggest things you can do to create wholeness within yourself. Changing your state of mind through movement and sweating, cold plunge, or sauna are all self-care practices that can change the emotional state in your body, so you feel at the highest vibration possible.

IT'S ALL IN YOUR CONTROL

When I played hockey growing up, I never trusted my abilities. I always thought I wasn't good enough, and I compared myself to others, thinking they were better and had what it took. Everyone talked about how it was one chance in a million to make it to the NHL, and that always made it feel so impossible.

I didn't have the mindset back then to realize that everyone has the same opportunity, and if you do your best in the present moment with the resources you have, that's all that matters.

One thing I wish I knew growing up is the importance of ownership and not blaming anyone else or any other circumstances for my shortcomings. Blaming the coaches, blaming other people, and being jealous of others' success is such a waste of time. I found myself lost in that world and giving away my power to it, instead of being real with myself and focusing on getting better in areas that needed improvement. I felt like I was owed something.

Entitlement is something you want to stay away from at all times. I wish I could have realized that. All I needed to do was to fully believe I could do it. I told myself this story that someone else had an edge and I didn't, which led to a further lack of focus. I deeply lacked that belief in myself; instead, the stories of how hard it was to make it always seemed to take over my mind. I thought someone just needed to believe in me or someone else on my team needed to score a big goal, because I didn't trust that I could do it, myself. I thought it was someone else's responsibility to fix the lack I had, instead of my taking ownership and focusing on the little things I could control.

Part of the lesson I'm trying to illustrate here is that taking complete ownership for your life and trusting in your abilities will lead you to where you need to be, even though you may sometimes experience self-doubt. We all get sucked into this Fixer archetype at some time or another. The key is to realize when we are in it and recognize how to get back into the Warrior. People who become successful in whatever field they choose don't focus on what others are doing or seek validation or approval; they do what they can to build the confidence, get super-focused on their intention and goal, and accept whatever will be will be. The problem in this case is that I spent more time trying to understand why things weren't working out rather than focusing on what I could do and what I could control in order to change the outcome.

We see this a lot in our world now. People are looking for everyone else to take responsibility for their health and their life. Not all of us, but a lot of us. People spend their days blaming the president, the economy, social media, whatever else. Most of the world is looking for someone else to blame or someone else to take responsibility for their problems, and they're wasting all their valuable energy instead of looking at their own lives and what they can control. What that does is take away their own innate power to change.

The only things we can control are what we do and how we react. Change happens when we all take personal responsibility to do the things that honor our truth. If you aren't in truth, you are living someone else's story, which is essentially a lie. If each individual person wasn't trying to get someone to fix them or their situation and instead focused on doing the work they needed to do, then slowly people would start to change. They would change how they look at life, how they speak, and how they behave.

When others see that you are a bit different and see a new light shining from you, see that you have been working on yourself and utilizing the life force energy you have to create a new life, they will suddenly feel inspired to do the same, because you are indirectly giving them permission. And at the end of the day, most people are just seeking a permission slip to do what they want to do but don't have the courage to do. So, if you are able to find it within yourself to make change and take complete ownership of your life, you will impact everyone else around you. When you do your best... like, your actual best... a sense of satisfaction flows in. It's like a pat on the back from the Universe saying, "Good job!" Do more of that!

Looking back, I used to feel a sense of regret because I never really gave my full 100-percent effort in anything. The days I did so in hockey brought me great results, but for many years, I half-assed things. I never really committed fully or burned the boats, so to speak. I would get an opportunity to rise to the next level, and for some reason, I'd talk myself out of it or tell myself a story about how there was probably someone else who could do it better.

This has happened for most of my life, with all the jobs I've had and career paths I've taken. I've had so many great opportunities that I let slip away, but I know now it was all for a reason. It's taken me a while to get over that, because I felt a sense of regret. But what I have realized is that those feelings are useless. Wallowing in the past and using the good old days as a way to cope with the present is natural, but it can be very unproductive if done for too long. I have learned that all those failed attempts happened to bring me here today. It's clear that my heart wasn't in those past opportunities, and I'm so grateful for that, because I would have been miserable.

Just shifting the perspective like that—to understand how all the things that didn't work out happened *for* you and not *to* you or *against* you—is now one of the most valuable lessons I've learned. This lesson has taken me out of victimhood and the Fixer archetype and into the Warrior energy the majority of the time.

Today, my perspective has changed, and my belief in myself has changed. I don't seek anyone outside myself to fix the shit in my life that I haven't healed yet or that I still struggle with. Yes, I may need support on things, but I know only I can take the action needed. I have done enough work now to know that I have grown enough and learned enough to get to the place I need to, at this point of my journey. I have realized that anything else is just procrastination or fear.

I also am aware that I am a student of life and will keep evolving and keep seeking the deeper truth within myself without doubting my abilities. In the process of writing this book, I have had to choose and decide that what I know is enough to help you transform your life. If I didn't trust in my abilities and my message, it would have been easy for me to give up.

The Fixer will show up in your life at some time or another, and that's okay. The key is to just understand, right now, that you are not broken, you aren't a victim, and you have everything you need to be whole within. The only one who can apply the knowledge, the tools, and face your fears and the unknown is you. The beautiful thing is you're not alone. We are all working through the same thing, just at different levels of our lives.

THE POWER OF INTUITION

Intuition is one of the most powerful forces we can tap into. It's an internal guidance system that connects us to our innate wisdom and inner truth. It can be one of the most challenging things to tune into, while also the most rewarding. It is the ultimate honoring of our truth. Awareness around the wounded mentality and behaviors of the Fixer is what allows us to move out of this shadow self. Intuition is the light archetype of the Fixer in that it moves us away from relying on external solutions and back into self-trust.

Usually, the message we receive through our intuition isn't the same as our most logical impulse. In fact, most intuitive hits defy logic. My theory is that the stronger the intuitive message you receive, the more challenging it will be to honor. That means willingly stepping into adversity or discomfort because you know, deep down in your heart, it's the right thing to do, regardless of how much you don't want to do it in the present moment. This can mean choosing the path of the unknown and having to trust that it will all work out in the end.

The concept of the higher self gets talked about a lot, but what does it actually mean? The higher self is a part of you that connects to a greater power, to spirit, or to an eternal source of energy, depending on what your beliefs are. This is considered a higher state of consciousness and allows you to connect to a deeper sense of awareness of yourself, which will open deeper insight into your desires, aspirations, and intentions.

I had heard the term and somewhat understood it, but it wasn't until my intentional experiences with breathwork, meditation, plant medicines, and psychedelics that I actually understood what higher self is and what it means to connect with it. This practice, made up of several practices, can really help you navigate your life toward fulfilling your purpose.

The challenge that can arise through this process is not knowing how to distinguish your ego and the stories that you tell yourself from the truth and the inner knowing of your soul, your true identity. In a noisy world, with a lot of distractions and a lot of stuff happening around us, it's very easy for us to get steered away from the truth; it's very easy for us to numb ourselves, to escape, to pretty much do anything other than allow ourselves to feel the deepest parts of our truth. Often, people live their whole life avoiding tapping into their inner knowing, because they're so caught up in the environment around them in reaction mode versus creation mode.

Your intuition often speaks to you in a whisper; sometimes, it'll get louder, and sometimes, your higher self will throw stuff in front of you to wake you up. Your intuition always knows the truth; your job is to be able to distinguish your logical mind (ego) from your internal heart compass, which is your higher self.

It's not about completely shutting down the ego, because this part of you plays an important role in creating safety between the heart center/desires and logical/moral perspectives, striving to satisfy immediate pleasure by causing the least amount of harm; in other words, finding the middle ground between your selfish, primal needs and what is deemed morally acceptable. But the ego can also stop you from listening to the truth. In order to distinguish between the two, you need to be able to quiet the noise around you and listen to your intuition.

Intuition comes from the heart. When you tap into your intuition, you are tapping into love. It's the truest form of who we are as humans. So, tapping into your intuition and that clear message you have from your higher self is essential for moving through adversity and aligning, during this part of the process. Because, if you aren't listening to your intuition, which is your soul, you are essentially living someone else's truth or someone else's life.

A lot of people learn stories and beliefs from other people, and we tend to live out those beliefs in our lives because they feel true to us; because it's what we've learned; because it's what the ego has constructed for us. But the problem is, if we aren't living in truth from our intuition, we're actually going further away from our highest potential, our purpose.

So, when you want to move through adversity, you need to ask this question, "Is this true for me? What can I learn from this?" If you are able to look at the adversity and tap into your higher self, your soul, your intuition, you will be able to get a clear message on what you'll be able to understand from the adversity that's in front of you; how it is going to be essential for your next level, even though, sometimes, it's going to be uncomfortable. Sometimes, that adversity is going to seem like a bad thing, but it's actually going to bring you rewards down the road. And that is why it's important to come from a place of love, which is your intuition, versus a place of fear, which is your ego trying to keep you safe. Distinguishing the two is very, very important for aligning and moving through adversity with the most empowered perspective.

Intuition speaks to you in ways that come from the heart, influenced by no one but your inner North Star. Sometimes, we feel a certain way in the moment, and it may be uncomfortable but in the long term will be more fulfilling to your soul and your higher self. We often search for pleasure in the short term, but in doing so, we may sacrifice the growth of our soul or our higher self in the long term.

I started to learn and understand what it means to connect to my higher self through several modalities that assisted me in arriving at the deepest parts of my inner-guidance system. I've been able to quiet the outside noise through meditation, breathwork, psychedelics, and plant medicine. Although I may have made some poor decisions at times, I have been really good at homing in on my inner voice, listening to it, and taking action, even when the message I received seemed crazy.

For example, when my hockey career ended, I felt a lot of pressure to jump into jobs that didn't feel right because they paid well. I was told to develop a trade. I was pressured into going to college to do something with my life. Even though going to college would have made things a lot easier in the short term, when it came to having conversations with people at family dinners or speaking to my girlfriend's family, I refused to ever do anything that didn't feel right in my heart and my gut. I tried many jobs that paid well, and I was miserable and depressed. I tried so many different roads, and nothing really felt good in my heart, until I found a job where I got paid and rewarded for serving people, and that's what led me to working in bars and restaurants, where I stayed for many years. Even though others may not have considered it the most honorable path, it was the one that felt right, and it led me to have the experiences and knowledge that brought me to where I am today.

Most people choose the known and the comfortable because they are scared of the unknown. One aspect of life where I have become skilled is learning to trust the unknown. If you want change in your life, you have to take chances and do things you've never done, trusting that the unknown will serve you in the end. This is where intuition comes into decision making. It is the tool I've used to gauge and measure how I make decisions. If you can understand this scale within yourself and really feel into it, it can change your life, and your decisions will bring more of life's rewards.

There are levels of impulse that you get from your intuition, and I rate these from 1 to 10. Your intuition always speaks to you in a whisper, but the volume of that whisper and the intensity with which it is felt in your body are correlated to the importance of the message. A level-1 whisper will be the quietest, and choosing to ignore this whisper likely won't be that consequential. A level-10 whisper will be a full-body experience that not only shows up as a loud whisper but a deep gut feeling or something you can feel intensely in your heart.

When you get a 9 or 10 out of 10, you need to take immediate action in some way, shape, or form, even if it's just writing it down or telling someone. These are messages that really matter and can make massive shifts in your life, and if you don't honor them, the universe will put things in your way until you decide to pay attention.

My theory is the more you ignore your intuition or fall off your true path, the more adversity you will face. You will learn the hard lessons until you decide to listen. If you answer the call of your intuition and must face adversity as a result, the outcome will bring you some kind of reward or opportunity.

Acting upon your intuition bravely is a trait of the Warrior archetype. When you know you must do something and it's a direct message from your intuition, you may be choosing the hard path, but the outcome will be different. You are consciously accepting adversity bravely. If you ignore your intuition, you will face more unexpected adversity down the road, without the reward, and will most likely not understand why this adversity has shown up. You will be stuck in the Victim archetype because you chose not to act in these situations.

There is something to be said for the power of feeling into your inner wisdom because doing so can influence the decisions we make and the outcomes we create in life. Most people seek short-term pleasure over long-term gain. Instant gratification is often counter to what we innately know is good for us. We are frequently pulled into this programming because it feels better quicker and, over time, builds a habit that favors dopamine over our greater vision. If you trust your intuition, you will see bigger results in the long term, even though it may not seem like it in the present moment, because of the challenge you face. Honoring the voice within is key to building trust in the outcome through any adversity.

I can think of two rock-solid examples of when my intuition whispered to me at a level 10.

Number 1 was starting my podcast. I remember thinking about it in 2018—about how badly I wanted to get my message out to the world and share my story. I remember thinking that I had this deep purpose within, that I needed to connect with people and make a global impact. I had no idea how that would happen, but when the opportunity to start a podcast presented itself, I knew right away, without a shred of a doubt, that I needed to do it.

I had one of those moments where I didn't care what it would cost and I didn't care what it would take. I just needed to make it happen. And when I made that decision, guess what happened? All the people and all the resources I needed showed up, and it all worked out.

When I realized that I didn't have the bandwidth to do it myself but loved the idea of interviewing people (likely from working in the bar industry for so many years), I found a team to do all the technical stuff so I could focus on my area of genius, which was the interview. This is what led to me founding my own company, Mic-Up, which helps visionary leaders amplify their brands, reach, and impact through podcasts.

This podcast helped me create my entire personal brand, helped take my confidence to a new level, helped me learn how to speak and communicate better, helped me build hundreds of relationships, and allowed me to have conversations with some of the most successful and inspirational people in the world. The crazy thing is, at the time, I had plenty of excuses I could have used, but the pull from my intuition was so strong, I couldn't even hear my inner critic at all.

If you have a strong enough pull and you believe in it enough and you feel it deep in your body and soul, nothing can talk you out of it. This is not to say, when you have such an undeniable desire, that it will come easy. This is all determined by the level of alignment you are in. Sometimes, it will be smooth—the more in alignment you are in your behavior and actions. Other times, it will feel like you have to bust through a brick wall, holding the reward of your vision on the other side. As you start to practice this and begin to get a better feel for what your ego is versus your soul—your intuition—the impulses you get will get easier to listen to and understand.

Through all the times I deeply wanted something, including starting my media company, I still had stories come up, but the belief I had in doing this outweighed any story I could create, and because of that podcast, I am able to sit here today and write this book. This is a prime example of a 10 out of 10 that completely changed my life.

And who knows what would have happened if I'd chosen to ignore that deep impulse... Where would I be? I guess we will never know. But what I do know is that many synchronicities took place after that decision, and I was rewarded greatly.

That doesn't mean I have been free of challenges or adversity. Challenges continue to test us as long as we continue to uplevel. However, I truly believe that the better you get at listening to your intuition, the less *unnecessary* adversity you will face. And when you do face adversity due to honoring your truth, you will be facing it head-on instead of running away from it.

A PROFOUND REMINDER

I had a profound experience on December 30, 2021. I was getting ready to wrap up the year and get some clarity for the year to come. It was late in the evening, and I was sitting in the small apartment I was renting with horrible Wi-Fi. I was in one of those moods. I was pissed off that the Internet didn't work properly, and I couldn't get a signal.

Then, I remembered I had one of Aubrey Marcus's latest podcasts downloaded and decided I'd watch that. This one was with Lukis Mac and his girlfriend, and they were discussing this new breathwork technique I hadn't tried yet. I was immediately motivated to attempt it. I won't go through the whole episode, but what I will tell you is the energy of these two resonated with me a lot, so as soon as the episode was finished, I knew I had to dive in.

This style of breathwork is pretty powerful. During the breathwork practice, after doing a full two rounds of the breath sequence, I was instructed to pause and ask my intuition, "What message do you have for me?"

And just like that, the information flowed in, like a giant wave from the ocean crashing down on a rocky beach. I had this profound reminder about why I am here.

My intuition told me I needed to stop messing around with the stuff that kept me from shining my light and stepping into my true power. It reminded me that messing around with things that dulled my light or got in the way of my mission was a waste of time. I had been drinking frequently, eating badly, not sleeping properly—all the things I already knew didn't serve me. The message was basically: "You know what you need to do. Stop fucking around."

It wasn't an aggressive message; the implication was, "You are in control. If you want to delay the process, go ahead. If you want to fast track it, start doing more of what you know works and less of the shit that doesn't."

The most powerful part of this was the message that came after that. "You don't have to struggle in this life if you don't want to. You have already endured enough pain and struggle in your past lives and have already been initiated into this one. So, you need to get that thought out of your head, that you need to keep struggling in order to make it in this life. You just need to believe and stop getting in the way of your own happiness and success... It's your choice."

As I dive deeper into this work within myself, I have started to believe more and more in past lives. My belief is that we chose to be here at this period of time, and that we carry deep insight, knowledge, and wisdom into this life from past ones or from our ancestors. I believe we learned profound lessons, and our life journey is to remember why we are here. I also believe that these deep impulses, or whispers of 9 or 10 out of 10 on the intuition scale, are linked to something in the past that reminds us of something we need to do, some synchronicity that is trying to tell us something now, in this life.

This is also why I believe we all have a Warrior deep within us. I believe we all have that inner Warrior who wants to be remembered and uncovered for whatever purpose you are meant to have in this life.

No matter what you believe about religion or reincarnation, I encourage you to just open your mind and heart and ask yourself what you think these powerful insights or gut instincts are. Maybe it's nothing. Who knows? But the more I learn and unpack this stuff, the more I feel that we are missing something here and need to go inward to look for the answers, rather than look outside ourselves.

INTUITION: THE ANTIDOTE TO THE FIXER

Intuition, looking inside ourselves, is a specific antidote to the Fixer archetype. The Fixer is a wounded archetype–someone who is always looking for the solution outside of themselves. So, in the case of the previous story, although I'm grateful that I watched the podcast that night, the podcast would have been useless if I didn't apply it right away in my own life.

The antidote to being stuck in Fixer mode and looking for answers outside of yourself is to take the empowered, opposite action and go inward, trusting your own innate wisdom. It's not going to always feel easy. Sometimes, sitting in stillness and doing breathwork hurts. You are literally choosing to step into adversity and the unknown. On the other side, however, is the light, which will bring you back into the energy of the Warrior, and you will experience less needless adversity later.

My theory is that the Universe will throw things in your way in an attempt to get you to pay attention and listen when you fall out of alignment. And this all starts when you ignore your intuition. The hard part is that most of us aren't aware of the trauma and stories we are living. And until you are willing to look at those shadow aspects of yourself–the trauma, the fears–and face them, they will always manifest in situations that are out of alignment, because the decisions you are making aren't coming from your truth; they are coming from these unaddressed traumas and stories.

We can learn all the information, but the only way to break free from the pain within is to face it. When you are able to sit with it, you will be able to trust yourself more. Then, when impulses come, instead of questioning or doubting yourself, you will be confident to answer the call and take the action needed. But this won't happen unless you are aware of and consciously move out of the dark aspect of the Fixer and into the light of your intuition.

For whatever reason, as children, at some point, we get conditioned out of imagination and into logic. Most of us were told to stop dreaming and start being practical. Teachers, parents, siblings, or anyone we looked up to had influence over how we felt about our choices, and sometimes those people convinced us that what we were doing wasn't right or that we didn't know something because we were "just a kid." The focus in our lives was going to school and then getting a job...

I was lucky in that I received a lot of encouragement from my family at a young age, and I was told I could do anything. It's probably why I have been able to find it within myself now to take the plunge to write this book and take on projects that I would have thought were crazy a few years ago!

My choice at the time was hockey, and because I had so much encouragement, I excelled at it. It wasn't until I was older—when I was bullied for the first time at my new school after moving across the country—that my belief system and confidence were destroyed. From there, the message I received was basically: "Make it as a professional or get an education, if you don't want to be a bum." As a teenager, feeling that pressure stops us from dreaming and following our hearts.

Because the world is all about consumption and making money, we are programmed into a system that gives us the tools to buy stuff. Our factory-style school system is set up so that, to be successful, you need to memorize the material and pass tests. That intuition, the light side of us, is darkened with the narrative that we need to abandon our dreams and make ourselves different (more logical, more employable, a better student); that we need to fix ourselves and the answers come from someone else.

I struggled for the majority of my life, not trusting that what I had to say was meaningful, and worried that, if I spoke up, people wouldn't take it seriously. I always assumed someone else's insights were better than mine, and I was afraid of being laughed at or thought of as stupid, so I didn't speak up in groups of people. In my teen years, it seemed to get worse and worse. It has impacted my life in all areas, and it's something I've struggled with, even up until now!

We all fall into the Wounded Cycle, but what is important to remember is that there is a Healing Cycle to apply.

BALANCING INTUITION & LOGIC

As a founder and CEO, having to make big decisions has challenged me because of my lack of belief in myself, which stemmed from when I was younger. What is important to note is, when it comes to business and entrepreneurship, you have to have discernment. You have to have a good balance of intuition and logic.

Of course, sometimes, we want to make the crazy, *big* decision, like an investment or other risk or commitment, and I believe action is key. But you also have to look at your situation and make sure that the decision does make logical sense at the time. Sometimes, you can take action on something slowly, in small bites; it doesn't have to be a massive, world-shaking decision overnight. As long as you make that decision and take at least a small bit of action, then it becomes real.

This has been challenging for me as an entrepreneur and business owner, because my choices affect the team and the business, so they really need to be thought out. I'll admit, this is definitely something I am still working on and believe I will continue to improve over time.

Through my personal development journey, I have gotten better at making decisions and trusting. Warrior energy is being able to make a decision and stick to it without fear, doubt, or lack of belief. I have learned, if I make decisions all from my logical mind and not my heart, then the outcome doesn't feel aligned. Something feels off. I find, if I have a good balance of intuition and logic, things will start to progress. Learning to make these balanced decisions from an entrepreneurial perspective is important.

What I notice is that, sometimes in the spiritual world, people get lost in the being and don't actually take any action, and they wonder why nothing is happening. There has to be a certain amount of aligned behavior and action to put your intuitive insight into action. Unfortunately, we can't just think or wish something into existence without some kind of action to follow.

Sometimes, we ignore our intuition and face adversity as a result. It will happen, and that's okay. That's how we grow. Every time that happens, we get a little wiser and a little better at stepping out of the Fixer, by applying our intuition, and into the Warrior.

MEDITATION

Meditation has been the most powerful tool I have been able to use to fully and purely connect to my intuition. Meditation is a tool that you can only cultivate within yourself (like breathwork). It is also one of the most challenging tools to master.

The reason meditation is so powerful and the reason it works is because you are getting out of your analytical mind and into your heart, connecting to your higher self. You are able to connect to different dimensions, and, essentially, you are able to change the energy within yourself. When you visualize exactly what you want to attract with the belief in your body that it's already here, it allows you to create a different reality. Your subconscious mind doesn't know the difference between what's real and what isn't. But it's not always easy.

As Dr. Joe Dispenza says, as you change your energy, you change your life, and if you are able to connect with yourself and get to the place where you are creating from a different dimension, from a different level, you are able to connect with the frequencies of that dimension and bring it all into reality. In the simplest terms, you're essentially just blocking out all external stimuli, all distractions, anything that would get in the way of you listening to your inner knowing and your inner voice. The challenging part of meditation is that you're constantly going to be bombarded with different voices in different parts of your ego that want to keep you from sitting still. The idea of meditation isn't to be perfect; it's just to notice and observe these thoughts that come into your mind, not as good or bad, just as they are.

At a retreat I attended in Sedona, every time I tried to meditate, I had this stupid fly buzzing in my face, and I just kept getting distracted, thinking, "Beat it, fly. Get out of here. Why are you here anyway?" I'd get up and move, and then I'd sit down, and it just kept following me.

Then it dawned on me: *The fly is never going away. The fly has just as much right to be here as you, so you need to accept the fly, because it's not going anywhere.* It was such a powerful metaphor for all of life's little annoyances and all of the things that are out of my control. There's never the perfect moment, so you have to sit still and learn to work with whatever is happening. And that's the beauty of it. It's being able to focus on what you need to do and to understand that it will never be exactly how you want it to be. The key is full surrender and acceptance. And as soon as I did that with the fly, guess what? It disappeared.

Meditation is a tool to help you to be present and centered so, when you do have these thoughts and when distractions come in and your mind decides to wander (this happens to all of us), you get better about bringing it back to your breath and back to center. This is why it can be useful in life outside of meditation—because there will be distractions or people or things that will try to pull us away from our centered, focused, present selves, especially when it comes to emotional triggers.

When meditating, it's okay to fall off for a moment, but the important thing is being conscious of that and being able to pull yourself back to center. Center represents our alignment in truth, like the guardian of your life that holds you in your fullest expression of light and love.

Because of the stories that we've created, the people we've met, and the experiences we've had, we've constructed these different narratives that get in the way of our truth. They become noise in our life, the clouded lens we see through, and it leads to us living a life of reaction. Our entire reality becomes based upon our external environment and what people are doing around us. What meditation does is allow you to essentially close that door to the outside world and connect inward to Source, God, the Universe—whatever you want to call the higher power that you believe in.

Another challenge that can present itself in meditation is what it can bring up. A lot of pain can surface, a lot of trauma, and a lot of emotions come up from sitting still and focusing. The idea is to improve each time, doing our best to embody, at least in the moment, the love you want to cultivate, the healing you want to take place, or the thing that you want to manifest.

It is clear that most of us are not programmed to sit still; we are programmed to constantly consume and do things to distract ourselves. We are often looking for some sort of reward or instant gratification, and this is a problem with our world. We are programmed to get what we want immediately, yet it is not usually the best thing for us. The best thing you can do is give yourself space to connect to yourself. As you start to connect to yourself, you start to cultivate more wholeness and love within your heart, which ends up changing the reality you see.

When you change what's going on inside you, the outside world looks different. You'll start attracting different things, you'll start attracting different people, and opportunities come knocking. Creating this peace within yourself is essential when you are moving through difficult times. You're essentially putting on your body armor for the day and developing that connection to your higher self so that, when things hit you throughout the day, you're already prepared for it. You may fall off, but you'll be able to come back from it much quicker and with far more ease and grace.

BREATHWORK

I've mentioned breathwork several times throughout the course of this book, but in case you aren't familiar with the practice, breathwork is a term for different breathing techniques where the conscious control of breathing can influence a person's mental, emotional, or physical state, which can bring a profound therapeutic effect.

Using breathwork to tap into your intuition is really powerful. Because you're focusing so deeply on the breaths in and out of your body, it allows you not only to be totally present but also to work through emotions in the physical body that can potentially block you from connecting to your intuition.

So, when you're able to breathe through the emotion and you're able to breathe through the discomfort, you are opening up a channel for yourself, to your higher self, to your intuition, because you've been able to work through the emotion and potential trauma that has been stored in your psyche and is surfacing during the exercise. While you're doing that, in addition, you're activating DMT, which you now know is like the radio signal in your brain that allows you to tune in to time, space, and other supernatural dimensions.

Breathwork allows you to create DMT naturally and open up your third eye, which detoxifies your pineal gland naturally through your breath. And if you do it properly, you can connect to a different dimension.

The first time I got to experience breathwork in person and with a group was in Sedona, Arizona, with Aubrey Marcus and the Fit for Service Fellowship. Aubrey Marcus is the founder of Onnit, a holistic lifestyle brand that specializes in total human optimization. He is the *New York Times* bestselling author of the book, *Own the Day, Own Your Life*, host of the *Aubrey Marcus Podcast*, and the founding member of the Fit for Service Fellowship. He has also been a key mentor in my life.

I discovered Aubrey in 2018, while listening to Tim Ferris's podcast. At that time, I was listening to a lot of Tim Ferris, as his book, *Tools of the Titans,* had a massive impact on my life in 2017. I remember seeing that Aubrey was, at the time, CEO and founder of Onnit, which was a company I had heard of through Joe Rogan's podcast and his flagship product, Alpha Brain. Joe Rogan is also a co-owner of Onnit.

Anyways, I was listening to this specific episode while on the treadmill, and I really resonated specifically with Aubrey's message. He was speaking in a way that really landed for me, and what he said was different from any of the other knowledge I was consuming at the time.

He spoke about things like philosophy, plant medicine, self-love—things that I hadn't heard too much about but knew mattered to me. Usually, you learn information about these sorts of topics from someone who dresses a certain way or is part of a certain subculture, but Aubrey was someone who I felt was similar to me. A regular fit dude, athlete, a guy's guy. I knew right away he was someone I needed to follow and learn more about.

So, from there, I went down the rabbit hole and discovered all of his work, and, shortly after, I bought his book. In 2019, he launched the Fit for Service Fellowship, which I almost did but backed out last minute. But I told myself, in 2020, when the Fellowship came around again, I was going no matter what, and it ended up being one of the best decisions of my life.

The group of coaches and the community was full of so many powerful humans who were all seeking truth and expansion in their lives, which led to many new relationships. We had our first summit in Tulum in February 2020, and then, *boom*, COVID hit. This threw a huge wrench in the plans, which led to us doing some meetups virtually.

Funny enough, this virtual meetup we had was the first time I ever did breathwork, and we practiced something called holotropic breathing. I had such a deep experience, I cried like a little baby. I released so much. I saw visions of my dad and went to another dimension. That virtual experience was very powerful, and it foreshadowed what was about to unfold later that year in Sedona.

Because we were mid-pandemic, traveling to the Sedona retreat was a challenge, but I knew, no matter what, I had to be there. My intuition basically said, "You need to do whatever is in your power to go there. Trust it will work." At the time, only essential travelers could leave the country, and I was worried that I wouldn't be permitted to leave. When I got to the border, I was completely honest. I told the border patrol agent I was going to a personal development event and that, for work, I had a podcast that dealt with mental health.

To my surprise and relief, the border agent said, "Wow, that's great! We need more people doing what you're doing. You may go ahead."

By the point when I got to the retreat, I had practiced breathwork several times, but this time was different. This breathwork practice, called Shamangelic Healing, was led by my now dear friend, Anahata Ananda. She was also a guest on the podcast, and you can check her out here.

Up until this point, I had only done virtual or breathwork by myself, so being in person in the Sedona desert with such powerful humans all around me... I knew I was in for a ride. When we started a session, I didn't feel a sense of sadness like I normally did. Instead, I almost immediately felt a sense of laughter and peace, and I began laughing out loud, even though I heard people crying and screaming. When you go deep into this practice, it really unpacks a lot of stuff that's hidden in there.

At one point, I felt my entire body step into this level of power I had never felt before. I had Kyle Kingsbury behind me. Kyle Kingsbury is a former UFC/MMA fighter and also the host of *The Kyle Kingsbury Podcast*. He looks like a modern-day gladiator and has the heart of a lion. He's also like a big teddy bear and one of the first dudes I'd seen who looks like he does express his emotions and cry in front of people, which helped me a lot when it came to self-judgment and expressing my truth to people. He is also one of the smartest and most well-read humans on the planet. You can check out our episode on the *University of Adversity* podcast here.

I remember this massive feeling of letting go, and then letting out this powerful force that felt like it had been stuck inside my body. I remember Kyle Kingsbury behind me telling me, "Let that fucking warrior out." I was in this trance, but I could still hear him. "Let that out, brother."

Then, I let that fucking warrior out. I let out a deafening roar, this gut-wrenching scream of joy. I was flexing my entire body like I was coming out of the movie *300* or *Gladiator*. It felt like I was being reborn, like I was releasing this Warrior within me who was fighting to come out. I suddenly felt so light. I was stepping into this Warrior power, this Warrior embodiment, like I was channeling an ancestor from a past life. I released the story that I was afraid of my power, and I became him.

Sometimes, that release is just what we need, and it has a profound ripple effect in our lives. What often happens with that release is that your body lets go of so much that is ailing it. When you have this stagnant energy inside of you, it can build up and make you physically sick. The energy needs to be released somehow.

In the past, breathwork was always very emotional, because I would see my dad and I was able to release so much, so many tears. It was really challenging but equally as powerful because, in the pain, I was able to let go and gain a connection with myself. It truly aligned me with my truth and the power I always knew I possessed within me.

CREATIVITY, ART, & PERSONAL EXPRESSION

The issue many of us face in Western society is our cultural values of materialism, achievement, and practicality. We are taught to go and do things that make money, that are in demand, and we are told to ignore our passions and not do things that aren't socially acceptable or "safe." We get into doing things that we don't really want to do to make money and to fit into a box. When we get lost in doing things just for money or to fit in, rather than seeking out what lights our soul on fire, we are destined to create a life and to attract people and circumstances that aren't really aligned with who we are. We aren't being true to ourselves. Even if, for the time being, you have to do a job you don't necessarily like, it's important to also give yourself space to tap into the creative flow and that communication with your higher self.

Our intuition or our higher self speaks to us through personal expression and creativity. Engaging in activities of creativity—making art, journaling, writing poetry, experiencing nature, making music, dance, and other body movement all hold the "being energy" or feminine energy of tapping into our creative genius.

The creative genius that we have within is our higher self. The doorway to our intuition, into our higher selves, comes in the form of these kinds of activities. They allow us to connect with ease and flow— the divine present moment. I'm sure at one point or another, even unknowingly, you've gotten lost in an activity where time doesn't exist, and you didn't have any judgment of what's happening or if it's right or if it's wrong; you just allowed the creative juices to flow. That is the most beautiful way we can express ourselves in human form. Everybody has their own way of doing this, which is so amazing, and that's why I encourage you to ask yourself, "What does this look like for me? What allows me to forget about the world around me?"

If we are able to harmonize the busyness of our lives, doing the job or the career that we have with our creative flow, we are going to be better at whatever job or craft we're working toward. Sometimes, we think that working harder and going after something harder is going to produce better results, but oftentimes, this is putting us in a state of lack, a state of control, a state of resistance. This is the unbalanced masculine at work. Rather, when we are doing something that taps into our creativity or into our flow state, it will allow us to embody the essence in our heart that creates powerful energy to attract what we want. Ideas will start to flow that could very well be better for your career or the craft that you are trying to home in on. You receive massive clarity on the path that most aligns with you.

Tapping into your intuition and your higher self is going to make you better at whatever it is you're doing. The challenge a lot of us face is that we don't allow ourselves to unplug from the go, go, go mentality and plug in to the slowed-down connection to ourselves. Engaging in creative activities is often a way to put us in a meditative state. If we open our hearts, we can discover there are so many things we love that light our souls on fire, allowing us to slow down and be with ourselves.

If you want to be able to move through adversity in a healthy way and escape the struggles that you are in right now, it's up to you to tap into your intuition as often and as much as possible. When we can quiet down the external environment and tap into our unique creative flow, then we are coming from a place of love, and that love is going to manifest in your reality. Odds are, when you allow yourself to step into this intuition, whatever path you're on gets clearer and easier because you've allowed yourself to listen to your higher self, to determine what it actually wants to create, which then allows you to solidify that in this reality.

When we close ourselves off to this connection with self, then we remain on autopilot, performing for the outside world and the demands of others. If you want to align with your higher self, it's imperative to take the time to sit in silence and think about what you love to do and what brings you into a Zen space and peaceful flow, then implement those things into your day.

This is guaranteed to improve the quality of your life, which, in turn, will improve your business, career, or whatever craft you are focusing on. In addition, this not only helps to heal past trauma, but it makes the moments of adversity you face that much easier to endure, which allows you to push through and come out stronger.

THE DISCIPLINE OF INTUITION

One of the challenges with tapping into our intuition is that we can have blocks, which are usually associated with trauma. These are the "emotional kinks" in the hose I referred to in Chapter 4. They prevent the flow of life from coming through us and keep us from tapping into our higher selves and the resources our souls provide.

Being able to work through the trauma and process your emotions will allow you to be able to get a clear connection to your higher self and to your soul. This connection helps us to release triggers caused by fear, shame, sadness, and all those other related feelings. In most cases, when you feel these emotions, it is because you've felt unsafe at some point in your life, so you use these emotions to protect yourself. Being connected to our intuition allows us to unlearn our stories and remember who we are.

There's a certain amount of trauma we go through that we can use in a positive way and that can drive us to use and channel it into creativity. The important point here is just to remember that our intuition is our highest self connected to God, connected to source, and the more we can open our hearts and connect and have heart and brain coherence, the closer we're going to get to our true path, our true purpose.

Ask yourself, "What kind of activities allow me to get into the zone, into my real truth, where I get out of my head and into my heart?" If more of us could ask ourselves this question and move through our challenges from that heart space, it would change the world.

PLANT MEDICINE: ANOTHER PATHWAY FOR TAPPING INTO YOUR HIGHER SELF

After a lot of thought and going back and forth on how I was going to write this section, I decided against covering each type of plant medicine and just focusing on my experience with Ayahuasca. Initially, I was going to speak to my experiences with each plant medicine I've used and explain the science and history behind each of their uses, but I felt I'd be doing you a disservice, as I am by no means an expert in this area and have only experienced psychedelics a handful of times. I do, however, encourage you to check out my podcast episodes that deal with these subjects and my experiences.

As I have continued to work on myself, I have felt less and less called to plant medicine and more to figuring out how to use my own body to connect with my higher self. I have been more focused on the integration of lessons learned and less on chasing the next experience. That being said, this medicine can be extremely helpful in certain times of your life, if used with reverence and respect. However, it can also bring challenges, if not used properly and with a trusted facilitator.

I am not encouraging the use of plant medicine, but I believe, if you are called to it for whatever reason, this may be able to help you connect with something deeper within yourself and facilitate deep healing.

The one story I will share with you is my experience with the medicine called Ayahuasca, because this illustrates a key decision I made in my life based on answering my intuition. This decision led to a lot of powerful insight and a new level of consciousness that changed my life forever.

Ayahuasca is a sacred medicine that is brewed as a tea and originates in the Amazon rainforest in South America. This medicine has been around for hundreds, some even say thousands of years, and it creates a powerful psychedelic experience.

The first time I heard about Ayahuasca was when Audrey Marcus spoke about it on Joe Rogan's podcast. This planted a seed of curiosity that stayed with me for a while. Then, when I learned that I had the opportunity to go on a retreat and sit with the medicine with Aubrey, who was one of my mentors, I knew I had to. That experience led to such a profound shift in my life. I also had the pleasure of sitting in the ceremony with his wife, Vylana, and a bunch of other amazing souls. This was a week-long retreat, and we sat with the medicine for four nights over a seven-day period, at Soltara Healing Center in Costa Rica.

What was really powerful was that, each night, we would set an intention, and that intention always showed up in some sort of experience, metaphor, or lesson that same evening. The medicine would last anywhere from four to six hours.

One thing I learned from this medicine is that you don't get what you want; you get what you need. And sometimes, when you think you have it figured out, the medicine will show you that you don't and force you to surrender and trust the process.

I recorded an episode with a full trip report that you can check out; it goes into all the details of each night. All nights were beneficial, but for me, the most powerful night was night four, when I got to see the depths of my full potential. I was able to tap into a different state of consciousness and see what was actually possible beyond my imagination and even this reality.

This opened up a deeper level of self-belief, which has stuck with me and has helped me in the work I do today. Without sounding too cliché, I saw that, if I stopped getting in my own way and fully believed in myself, there would be literally endless possibilities and success to be created in my life, but I was the only one who would stop me from getting there.

When Aubrey, Vylana, and I had finished our ceremony that night, we went onto the star deck, which was a great big patio overlooking the ocean, and we basked in the magic of nature and the stars. Late into the night, you could hear the animals' voices yelling in the distance, almost as if they were communicating with one another. The sky was lit up very brightly, and it was the first time I had ever looked at the sky with such curiosity and awe. Each night, Vylana or my dear friend Steph sang, which helped us all peacefully absorb what had just happened in ceremony.

On this night, as I sat on the star deck, looking at the stars, all of a sudden, my heart started to race. I could feel my body starting to activate again, like it had when I took the Ayahuasca earlier, and panic set in. *Oh shit, not again!*

As I sat there in a panic, feeling like I was being taken into another world and like my body was fading away, Aubrey said to me, "You okay, brother?"

I said, "Bro... I'm in it again. It's reactivating."

Right then, Aubrey put his arms around me, put his hand on my heart, and helped me breathe through it. Then, Vylana started to move around my body, waving her hands around like she was moving energy, and while she was doing that, she sang a beautiful song. She became this different creature, who looked like the character Neytiri from Avatar. It looked like she was performing magic.

It was one of the wildest things I've ever experienced. I felt like I was in a different world and felt such peace. They continued for a few minutes, and after that, I felt a calm energy radiate through my body, and I was back. I was still in the medicine but not in a panic. I felt a comfortable sense of control. I then went back to my room, put on some music, and danced the night away, because I had this incredible buildup of energy like I was going to explode. The love I felt for myself and my being was something I had never felt before.

I will never forget that night, because it changed my life forever. I looked myself in the mirror, and, for the first time, I saw myself as someone would see me upon meeting me, and I respected myself like they would. It's hard for me to put into words what it feels like to see yourself that way—the way others see you—but it helped me create a level of self-love, self-respect, and self-belief that wasn't there before. (Now, I don't know if this is how other people actually see me, and I never will, but that was the feeling I got, and that's what was important in this context.)

I saw myself without my own personal stories or judgements of my past. It was like I was actually looking at myself for the first time in my life, and a message came to me saying, "This is how people see you." Hearing that and feeling that has changed the way I'll see myself forever. Being able to see into this kind of perspective has helped me look past my doubt, negative self-talk, and a lack of belief. The lesson I learned from this experience was profound enough that, when I start to fall into that downward spiral of self-doubt, I can put myself back into that moment, and it helps me remember to get back into the groove I need to be in.

I believe plant medicine works as a bridge to our intuition and our innate wisdom—a level of consciousness that we may not have had access to or even known was there. When you have a strong pull to the medicine or you have been called to this medicine, that is a sign that you already know there is something deeper; you just don't know what that is. And the more you explore yourself and, potentially, these medicines, the clearer the information becomes, which leads to a deeper level of connection and understanding of yourself.

This quote was one that came to me to summarize this medicine and the experience I had: "A symphony of dark and blissful chaos." If you feel intrigued to learn more about my Ayahuasca journey, you can tune in here:

CHAPTER 10

STEP #5: ALCHEMIZE

al·chem·ize:
> transform the nature or properties of (something) by a seemingly magical process.

This is the point in the journey of adversity when we move from going inward with ourselves, stepping into belief and aligning in our highest identity, to actually moving into action and integrating everything we have become. This last step is a critical piece in the journey because, without it, nothing would change.

This is where the fun starts. We are going to take what we've learned and act on it. I love the word "alchemize" because it really is a spiritual and magical practice—bringing something to life. Being able to take different ideas and knowledge and turn them into something real and tangible. It's great to learn different things, absorb different ideas, and use different tools, but when we alchemize it into action and face adversity head-on, that's when it all matters.

I wanted this book to be a personal development and growth tool combined with the spiritual essence of alchemy that you can apply to your life, so you can transform any adversity you encounter because you're essentially mastering yourself. We've gone through the steps. You've learned. You've grown. And now, when you look at the adversity in front of you, you can turn that situation into a gift you can be grateful for later.

You can do all the reflecting, meditating, spiritual breathwork, and psychedelics you want, but if you don't take all of that and apply it to your everyday life, in the present moment, in step-by-step action, then it's useless. Actually doing and taking action in this reality can be one of the most challenging aspects of this process, though, because you're going to face a lot of resistance. There is no fulfillment or reward without a price.

The actual feeling of taking action here, of alchemizing all that you've learned and then going for it without looking back, is going to feel uncomfortable, but just know, on the other side of that, you are going to be rewarded.

ALCHEMY IN ACTION

I have had to fight through my own adversity in order to alchemize this very book you're reading. You see, growing up, I was typically one of the smarter kids in class. I was usually an honors student and considered a very good writer for my age. As a young boy, I showed a lot of promise as an academic, but as I got older, that slowly started to fade away. Things seemed to get more challenging for me in school. I'm not sure if that's because school was just easier from kindergarten to sixth grade, but as soon as I got into seventh grade and through high school, academics became a lot more challenging for me.

I really started to notice it when I had to move across the country and go to a new school. Not only was the schoolwork challenging, but I also struggled to meet new friends. I didn't want to be at school and I just stopped caring. Whenever I could get away with missing class, I would. Six months in that school being bullied was really hard on my confidence, and I just stopped giving a shit about my classes. I managed to get by, but as I got older and into high school, my lack of regard for academics had solidified, and my ability to learn and retain information wasn't there.

I struggled in high school and basically cheated my way through every exam I could. I never felt inspired at school and always felt zoned out. I wasn't motivated at all and was stuck in la-la land. I spent my time chasing girls and playing hockey because that's where all my validation came from. There was also so much family stuff going on, it really distracted me from caring about academics.

I always loved writing, but because my structure and punctuation were so bad, I always got terrible grades. I lost interest and stopped trying. When I prepared and did my best, I still got shitty grades, so I started to think I was dumb.

This has been a lifelong challenge, something I have had to deal with even when writing this book. The belief I needed to have within myself to see myself as someone others would consider worthy of writing a book did not come easy. I knew, if I wanted to make it happen, I needed to follow my own steps. I needed to continue stepping into awareness of why I felt doubt, dive into deeper healing work around where this came from, so I could move through it, step into unwavering belief that this was possible, align my environment and intuition with no other outcome than the one I wanted, and step into radical action to become that published author I always knew I would be.

I knew I needed to step into this identity and this outcome as if it had already happened. So, day in and day out, I did the things a published author would do—I took care of my body and mind, I stayed disciplined in my daily writing ritual, I hired a writing coach to keep me accountable, I hung images of my book cover in my home, and I spoke everything I wanted into existence.

Whenever thoughts of "Who is actually going to care about this book?" arose throughout this process, I was able to quiet them by remembering that, when we speak from the heart, we can move mountains. When we speak from truth, everything flows to us with ease and grace. We can do no wrong when we tap into Source and act from our open heart. Our instincts never lie, and I knew my instincts would never fail me. I believe that words are medicine. My drive to deliver this message far outweighs my doubts about how it would happen or if it would be "good enough."

The journey of bringing this book to life was one of my biggest lessons in letting go. We so badly want to control everything. We think it helps create our best outcome. But the irony of this is, we create the most fulfillment and impact when we trust and surrender. Complete surrender isn't about giving up. It's about doing your best and giving the rest up to the Universe, trusting that everything will fall into place exactly as it's meant to.

And here we are today.

One more thing. I recently learned that, when it comes to learning, there is another factor at play. In 2018, I got a brain scan done by my good friend and amazing naturopathic doctor, Dr. Nicholas Jenson, at Divine Elements in Vancouver. The scan said my prefrontal cortex was operating at a 2 out of 10. The struggles I've gone through turned out not just to be in my head... no pun intended. This functional deficit may have come from many years of partying or from getting punched in the head in hockey or bar fights. The uncertainty of the root cause has definitely played on my mind. I know I can get my brain to perform when I need to, but I often wonder what my brain would be like if it were firing at a level 10.

During a deep magic mushroom trip, I was also told by my higher self that I had been living with a learning disability my whole life. When I received that message, it all started to make sense. I always wondered why it was so hard for me to stay focused or absorb new information easily. Even when reading, I would sometimes have to read a passage over and over again. When I think back to my brief semester in business school, I remember spending hours and hours after school to learn business math, and then I would take the test and get like thirty percent.

For so many years, I've wondered if something was wrong or if it was just a story. Now, while writing and sharing this, I am forcing myself to break through the barriers of limitation, through the beliefs that I can't write a book, that I can't learn. Even if I do have a learning disability, I will continue to lean into it and do the best I can, because, in my heart, I know that getting this book into the world was worth more than listening to a story that may or may not be true. The power of resilience and perseverance has allowed me to work through my own personal adversity to bring this thing to life.

A NEW PERSPECTIVE: THE WARRIOR & HEALING THE SELF

I will be honest with you. Writing about this archetype has given me the most resistance.

The interesting thing is, this entire journey, from starting to finishing this book, has forced me to look within the deepest level of soul and tap into the Warrior energy spirit I know I have and that we all have. I have watched myself fall into the Victim, the Distractor, and the Fixer over the past year in the process of bringing this thing to life.

Embodying the Warrior doesn't mean perfection; it means being aware and choosing who you want to be, when you are challenged or put in a difficult situation. And always from a place of love, not fear. All of us fall off the path and into these different archetypes, but what really matters is how long we stay off the path before we come back into our power.

You see, we all have the Warrior spirit within us. My goal is to help you realize that within yourself and to help you unlock it, so you can practice embodying it in all areas of your life. This process can be fucking hard and will force you to take a really honest look at your behavior, your habits, your beliefs, and your mindset, but I promise you, when you start to get super-clear on what a Warrior is versus what a Warrior is not, you will start to connect to that true Warrior essence that you were born to access.

It doesn't matter your race, your sex, your skin color, your background. What matters is that you are able to search within yourself and look beneath the wounds and the stories of the past to uncover the truth. As I've said before, our families and our ancestors survived incredibly challenging situations for us to be here right now today, so I want to honor that and acknowledge what a privilege it is to not only exist but to grow.

I began writing this book in March 2021 and completed it in March 2022, but the idea started long before that. The world has been faced with some very difficult times, which have forced a lot of people to look at themselves and step up in their lives or let go of things and make some difficult choices that may involve a serious pivot. Embodying the Warrior is not only applicable during a pandemic; it is important going forward for all the adversity you will face in the future. How you navigate and face adversity will determine the life you create, and if you can embody the Warrior for the majority of your human experience, you will create a fulfilling life.

I have had to ask myself many times over, "Who do I want to be?" Do I want to show up as the angry, wounded, resentful, victimized, scared little boy? Or do I want to show up as the empowered, loving, resilient, compassionate human being who listens to my inner knowing and the wisdom of my intuition?

When I made the conscious decision to choose the Warrior, I had to go deep into getting clear about what that meant for me, and then understand my patterns and tendencies that would bring me closer or further away from the Warrior archetype.

I realized I had a lot of work to do to become the man I wanted to be. It wasn't that there was something wrong with me or that I was broken, but I knew, within my soul, I wasn't living up to my full potential, so I had to get clear on why that was. As I started to study more and learn from mentors like Aubrey Marcus, I started to see and feel what empowerment from a place of love versus fear actually means. With that came the ability to stand up for what I believed in, have open and vulnerable conversations on my podcast, and show up from this place of truth rather than doubt.

What do I mean by that? Say, for example, I was doing a post on social media. First, I'd ask myself, "What is the purpose of this post? Is my intention to inspire people to think critically and empower them? Or is it to seek a reaction and stir the pot with no action steps, leaving those who read it angrier and worse off? Would this post inspire me? Or am I trying to get a reaction?"

If the answer didn't feel right in my gut, I would delete it or change it to something that may still pull some emotional strings but would also empower people, so they felt more elevated to actually make a change in their lives or think differently, not just add fuel to the fire and make them feel more down and deflated.

This is one aspect of the Warrior that you can apply right now when it comes to your interactions with others. It is a very simple way for you to embody love rather than fear. Our decisions have to come from the right place; they can't just be reactions to other people or circumstances. This is why getting clear on our intentions and getting rock solid in our beliefs is so important. When shit hits the fan or someone triggers you emotionally, you want to make a decision that is true to you, not a reaction of emotion to someone else.

We see this all over the place in our society. True Warriors understand the value of being patient, gathering all the intelligence available, and making the best decisions that are closest to their heart and intuition. You don't need to be a samurai or a Spartan to do this; we can all do this right now.

There is a simple but profound quote from Ram Das, which he learned from his mentor: "Love everybody, and tell the truth." This is not an easy thing to do, but it is powerful.

If you can love everyone as a soul, as part of you, then you are coming from a place of love. Judgment will always happen, and that's okay; it is the endeavor itself to love everyone that is important. When you attempt to love everyone where they are at and for the human they are, even if you disagree with them, you embody what it is to be a true Warrior in this context.

This doesn't mean you have to go around telling everyone you love them. This doesn't mean you should be weak and take shit from people. What this means is that this person you disagree with was once a young child just like you, and they most likely have a difficult story and a set of problems they are working through as well. Be curious. How did they become that way? How much pain have they had to go through to become that way? Maybe they're pissing you off, and maybe their actions are triggering to you, but the problem is, if you judge them or hate them and feed into that energy, you are only causing more pain for yourself and the people around you.

This can also be said about holding grudges. There is that famous quote, "Holding a grudge for someone is like you drinking poison and expecting the other person to die." That person will never feel your pain, so you are only wreaking havoc within yourself by holding on to the hate, resentment, or grudge.

As I write this, I'm thinking to myself, *Lance, you're not even doing this in your own life...* And you know what? I don't always do this in my own life. I go down the judgmental anger spiral, too. I'm human, as are you. But... I'm a lot better than I was before, and the fact that I'm aware allows me to get better at it.

So, just think about that today. Whenever you hate or judge, you essentially are only hurting yourself, as life is just a mirror and a reflection of what's going on inside you. There are some really disturbed people in this world doing terrible things, no doubt about that. But if we focus on them and we feed hateful and resentful energy, we are only robbing ourselves of our own power and high-vibrational energy.

Telling the truth seems so simple but is one of the hardest things to do. Telling the truth doesn't just involve directly lying to others; it also involves avoiding telling the truth and lying to ourselves. We tell ourselves small lies in order to eliminate short-term awkwardness, but most of the time, this just leads to long-term difficulties. If we can work on being a bit more honest every day and not avoiding the difficult truth or conversation, I believe we save ourselves a lot of headaches down the road.

EMBODYING THE WARRIOR WITHIN

As I sit and write this book, the world is full of chaos. The narrative that has been presented about the COVID-19 pandemic never sat right with me. It's not about whether it was correct or incorrect; in my heart, it just didn't *feel* right. In 2020, when this all started, I had to lean into myself and ask my intuition what the right move was.

During the pandemic, the world was flipped upside down, and our lives changed right before our eyes. We all did our part in hopes of bringing the craziness to an end. We were told we couldn't travel, and that all made sense, until it started to become apparent that travel restrictions weren't actually doing much to bring the number of infections down. There was a point around September when I started to question whether or not what was going on actually made sense to me and if continuing to follow these guidelines would eventually do more harm than good. Reports were surfacing that the rates of mental health issues, domestic violence, teen suicide, and drug and alcohol abuse were skyrocketing.

Now, I want to preface this discussion by saying everyone has been on a different journey through this pandemic, and I'm not here to say whether or not what I did was the right way or the wrong way. It's not a debate, and I think you will understand this by the end.

I simply want to give you my perspective on how, in my personal environment, I had to embody the Warrior spirit for fulfillment of my purpose. It didn't come easy.

But something in September changed it all. Because I had this one realization, the entire trajectory of my life shifted.

As I mentioned earlier in this book, there was an opportunity to go to Sedona for a retreat and then to a separate healing retreat in Cosa Rica in January 2021. I knew I had to be in Sedona and Costa Rica. No matter what, I was going to figure out a way to get there. That's how strong the pull was.

Remember when I talked about the intuition scale? When I saw this opportunity come up, this was a 10 out of 10. I felt a deep calling within my gut and my heart. It was a message that this was a *must do*. I knew, no matter what, I had to figure it out and make it happen. I was also getting a lot of synchronicities telling me that I had to go to Costa Rica. It would come up in conversations with others and during meditation.

Paying attention to your intuition and not gaslighting yourself into thinking it's not real is very important. When you're not trained to listen to and act on your intuition, there is a tendency to talk yourself out of whatever it is guiding you to do or to question its authenticity. This is what stops people from moving forward and creating change or new opportunities in their lives.

Synchronicities are real, and we must pay attention to them. Listening to your intuition is a key trait of the Warrior archetype. We discussed intuition in the Alignment chapter as the antidote to the Fixer, but since this concept is tantamount to embodying the Warrior in general, I would like to reemphasize it here. I believe that neglecting this ability is what keeps a lot of people from greatness.

You've got to get super-skilled at listening and feeling the messages your body is giving you without fear, doubt, or worry getting in the way of you taking action. When I saw this opportunity to go to Costa Rica, I knew I needed to make this happen no matter what. So, I cleared up my credit card and bought the spot immediately. This way it was real. Right after I did, though, all of the stories came up... *Wait a minute—we are in a pandemic! How are you going to leave?* Every worry and excuse in the book came up, and I said to myself and my inner judge, "We will figure it out." And I did.

As I look back on 2021, the year that followed that retreat, it really was one of the wildest years of my life. I had to face both polarities of myself. The first half of the year, I was sober in Costa Rica. I had no temptation to party, and I just wanted to live in the jungle and focus on work. The other half of the year, I was faced with my dark side. After nine months, I fell off sobriety in Miami and later ended up in Mexico. This was also a place I was called to through my intuition and another example of a situation in which I needed to answer the call and embody the Warrior spirit. This choice meant a lot of change and major uncertainty, and, of course, it wasn't easy.

On October 29, 2021, I sold everything I owned, including all my furniture, electronics, and even my Jeep that I loved so much—everything except for a suitcase of clothes, a laptop, and podcast gear—and I moved to Mexico. To be honest, I had no idea why I was being called to move there. A lot of people were shocked, but most understood.

After being back in Canada for a couple months and after spending all of August writing the majority of the first draft of this book, I started to lose motivation. It was an incredible feeling to write a book, but I was plagued with all sorts of negative self-talk: "I'm not capable of writing a book," "No one will care," all the excuses... I started to question whether Vancouver was the place I was really supposed to be. The comforts of my apartment, my furniture, my computer, and my Jeep were great, but I could feel myself losing steam and falling into a world of laziness. I felt very out of alignment with my environment.

Much of the craziness going on didn't align with my values. I was troubled by the policy changes and bizarre mandates. The key point here is that, as Warriors, we have to understand and listen to what feels right to us and discern whether it is in alignment with our values and our purposes. This isn't about picking sides about what is right or wrong, and it's not political. It's about getting super-clear on what feels right to you and making sure the choices you make are from your heart and not from other people's opinions.

This is one of the hardest steps to embodying the Warrior. You must learn to get quiet and listen to what feels true to you. Sometimes this will mean going against the majority. This may bring a lot of discomfort in the present, but it will bring a lot more long-term satisfaction to your heart. For me, it wasn't just the pandemic and all of the circumstances surrounding it that were the issue but a general feeling of misalignment. I desperately needed clarity, and the next thing gave me just that.

I had been aware of a pretty well-known medicine called Kambo for quite some time; it is also known as the vaccine of the Amazon. This non-psychoactive medicine comes from a toad in South America and has powerful cleansing effects. It has been used for thousands of years.

A friend of mine had mentioned it to me and recommended I try it, because she knew I was seeking clarity and wasn't sure which direction to take in life. Now, I'm not saying you need to take a medicine like this if you don't have clarity; what I'm saying is that you need to find what works for you at quieting the noise and figuring out a deeper connection to your intuition, Universe, or God. It really doesn't matter what you want to call it; the main point is that you are connected to a higher power and that power is communicating important information to you. If you can get quiet, you will be able to receive the message you need. I felt the call to do this medicine, because it is known to deliver a heavy detox, purify your body so that you can be a clear vessel, and give you maximum clarity to connect deeper to the message you need to feel into.

After going through three rounds of the medicine, I purged more than I ever have before. It was one of the most brutal experiences, like having the world's worst flu hit me like a ton of bricks. My whole face swelled up, my eyes watered, and I felt intense discomfort in my gut. I hated every second of it, until it was over. I had completely underestimated it and never thought it would hit me like that. I also didn't follow the proper diet beforehand, which I highly recommend you do, if you try this stuff. It depleted every bit of energy out of my body. I felt deeply disoriented and stuck, like it would never end.

After the last round, the most blissful feeling of a calm and clear mind set in. It was beautiful even though it was painful. The bliss afterward made it all worth it. I asked myself, "Okay, now what?" Nothing really surfaced until a couple days later.

I was walking to get groceries for dinner, as was my routine pretty much every day, and out of nowhere I had this profound flow of information into my body. This came from the question I had asked after taking the medicine: "What direction am I supposed to take next? Where am I supposed to be?"

I wasn't being pulled back to Costa Rica, but I did get the feeling I needed to go somewhere. Beforehand, Mexico was somewhere I had considered going to visit, but it wasn't somewhere I'd thought I would move to.

The 10-out-of-10 impulse came like this.... "You need to sell all your things and move to Mexico. If you want to allow new energy and opportunity to flow into your life, you need to let go of this stuff that is holding you back."

A couple years prior, I had bought a Jeep and a bunch of furniture. I had felt for a while that I needed to let go of this stuff at some point, but it wasn't until this moment that I felt it was completely necessary. I also got this download that told me I was trying to hold on to the past and trying to recreate something that I'd had years before, and it was just not going to happen.

Vancouver was the city I had lived in from 2007 to 2012, and I'd had some wild and crazy times there before selling everything at the end of 2012 and moving to Australia. What the new message was telling me was that I needed to let go of the thought that this was the only place I could call home. I'd always had one foot in and one foot out, which had caused me to feel stuck energetically. I knew Vancouver wasn't where I was supposed to be at this moment in time, but I kept telling myself this story that it was. Once I had been away for seven months in 2021 and gotten settled back in, it didn't feel right.

The main message I now had was that I needed to let go of this place and let go of what was keeping me attached to it, because if I did, it would allow me to free up space energetically and allow new opportunities and people to flow in. Part of embodying the Warrior spirit is knowing when to let go of things, even if it feels uncomfortable, and this message told me to sell everything and move to Mexico. I asked myself, *Does this feel true to me?* When I sat with it, a surge of energy and excitement flowed in, and that's when I knew it was the right move.

Then I thought about how much money I'd invested in the furniture and my Jeep; I'd surely take a big loss. That part bothered me, but when I took the financial side out of the equation, the feeling of letting go was a relief. It can be so easy to talk ourselves out of things when it comes to money and possessions. These things can weigh us down. Our clothes, possessions, cars—these things become a part of our identities. In this way, letting them go means part of you has to die. However, what I've noticed is that letting go of possessions may sting at first, but the freedom and clarity it brings in energetically is priceless. I'm not saying owning stuff is bad or having a great place with amazing furniture and decor is bad; what I am saying is, if the stuff in your life is holding you back from exploring your purpose and your truth, then maybe it's time to let it go. We can always buy new stuff, but we can't buy more time here on this Earth.

Mexico is full of temptation, fun, and freedom. One challenging aspect of moving to Mexico is that I've been forced to look my shadow side in the face—the partying, the drinking—and embrace it. My old lifestyle is something I've been hiding from and fighting, and I was called to a place that forced me to stare it in the face every single day.

I've had to face both polarities of my life in 2021, from complete healing and sobriety in Costa Rica to falling back into old habits and partying in Mexico. I have had to force myself to figure out the balance, because, for the first three and a half months in Mexico,

I struggled to stay sober for longer than two weeks. But I also feel that was for a reason.

Now, I am happy to say as I finish writing this book, I am two months sober and will continue for the rest of year and possibly longer. So, like I mentioned, while writing this book, I was forced to go through the entire framework myself and apply it in real time! I am not just saying this; I am actually practicing it as I bring it to life on the page. I have had to go into the dark places of mental hangover and dig deep into the emotions I have felt. I have laughed and I have cried a few times over trying to get a grip on what my actual balance is. Do I kill my old partying identity and deny part of who I am? Or do I work with it and work on balancing it into the life I've worked so hard to create?

Writing this book has brought forth a wave of emotions, but as I sit here writing about the Warrior archetype, I realize that this is what is truly at the core of this work. For me, embodying the Warrior archetype has been the full exploration of myself—digging into the dark spots, accepting the dark and my shadow as an important part of who I am, and loving it with as much love as a person would love a family member they cared about. Then it just becomes a question of: Who's going to sit at the head of the table? Who's going to sit at the throne of my life? This is where I've had to decide what that means to me and what I need to do in order to stay true to myself, keep balance, and be able to show up energetically the best I can for my team and the people in my life.

I believe one of the reasons I was called to Mexico was to experience this polarity, to face this temptation, and to learn to navigate it while running a company, hosting a podcast, writing a book, working on a TEDx Talk, and everything in between. I'm sure there are other reasons, too, that will unfold soon.

Throughout the process of writing this book, I have been confronted with every excuse and every story of the past telling me I'm not a writer, that I'm not smart enough, that I've failed so many times at so many things, that my learning disability would stop me, that I wasn't worthy of writing a book... You name it, and I thought it. Every single story and excuse have hit me, and I've had to dig deep and ask myself, "What's actually true? If I don't write this book, if I don't bring it to life because of my fears or limiting beliefs, who am I robbing of my message?"

"Someone needs to hear this message." This is what I tell myself when these stories and excuses emerge. "It would be selfish of me to quit because of these excuses, if someone desperately needs to hear this message and won't receive it because of the fear and the stories."

Now, I recommend that you take this into consideration. Maybe there is something in you, in your voice, in your mission, that someone out there needs. This is a big part of unlocking and embodying the Warrior—listening to that and being able to trust that what you have to say matters and that someone out there will connect with it. This is one of the true staples of being a Warrior—speaking your truth despite your stories and your judgmental inner critic. It's about listening to the truth and what really matters and learning to get out of your head and into your heart because the world needs you.

Warrior energy is powerful, but it's not perfect. It's complete self-awareness and having a true understanding that what you see in the outer world is a direct reflection of what's going on in your inner world.

The better you can get at deep, honest self-exploration, the better you will show up as the empowered Warrior you are. When you can do this consistently, that adversity in front of you will simply be one more puzzle piece of your life that you are ready to dance with, and it won't seem nearly as daunting as it once did before.

CONCLUSION

During the COVID-19 pandemic, I realized that we live in a world full of traumatized people. It's not anyone's fault, but, as a whole, I've noticed the majority of our world operates out of fear. When we are in fear, when we are divided, we are more likely to give away our power to something outside ourselves. If we are whole, if we have unity and all have love for one another, then we won't rely so much on others to help us feel safe. Unfortunately, that wouldn't be profitable for those who appear to be raking in boatloads off of our collective fear.

Throughout this time, I have also noticed that we tend to believe things based on our past experiences, the environment around us, and the people we follow on social media. Even though something might not completely resonate with our hearts, we tend to align ourselves with a political agenda and their narrative, because the payoff is some type of reward, whether that be safety, certainty, or a sense of belonging. My intention here isn't judgment—we all fall into this trap— however, I do feel it is important to point out these observations.

When we aren't diligently connecting with our inner self, we tend to parrot the ideas and opinions of those we're closest to or those we listen to as authorities. This becomes dangerous, because we don't end up thinking for ourselves and listening to our hearts. The majority of the choices being made by those in power on varying ends of the political spectrum are not coming from a place of love; they are based on figuring out how to create the most fear possible, because, when we are in fear, we are willing to spend more money on fixing the problem to find a solution.

I've realized over the past two-plus years that creating change and inspiring somebody to think differently will never come from shaming or guilting them. We've stopped listening to where other people are coming from. There has been a lack of empathy, compassion, and love among all people during this pandemic, and that is where the problem lies. There are too many people pointing fingers and telling people how to think and who to trust and how to live their lives based on their own personal opinions.

But the reality of it is: Why does any particular individual's opinion matter? Why is what they say the be-all and end-all? They are only basing the way they think on the knowledge that they've been shown in their particular life and on the people they associate with. So, the question is, who's right?

The answer is: nobody. Everybody is just basing how they think and their opinions of the world on their past stories and how they've lived life up until this point. As you've learned throughout the course of this book, we are all impacted by our past adversity and trauma, and these things shape our opinions and behaviors in the present.

The world would be a completely different place if we woke up to what each of us have, individually, created in our lives and took responsibility for our own healing—healing that embodies love over fear.

Have you ever wondered what the world would be like if we actually spent time trying to understand the opposing opinion, instead of telling somebody that they're wrong or that they should think a certain way or do a certain thing? What if we genuinely got curious about why people think differently from us, without judgment?

Instead of spending our precious energy telling others how to act, we can change our very reality by focusing our energy on how we can better show up for ourselves and others.

When you wake up in the morning, I want you to ask yourself:

What are you thinking about?

Are you thinking about how you can show up in the world and how you can cultivate better energy so that the environment around us can benefit?

Or is your default to wake up in reaction mode?

Do you want your life to be constantly dictated by the environment around you?

Our phones, social media, our neighbors, our family, whatever it is—it's a choice, whether you create your own reality in your own life and focus on yourself or whether you allow the other people and other things to control your reality. You're either in the driver's seat of your life or you're in the passenger's seat. Which one do you want to be in?

In order to really get to the root of the problem and move forward to actually make change, we must focus on our individual selves and how we show up every single day. We have no control over anyone but ourselves, but we can inspire others. The energy you create within your body has a frequency that impacts the outer world around you. When you change your energy inside, you change your life and your perspective. If we focus on ourselves and how we show up in our energy, then we will become empowered in our own lives and empower others through our influence.

This is an opportunity for unity. This is an opportunity for people of different opinions to come together and learn from and help heal one another. If we can have compassion and understanding and truly support others where they are at, we have a bigger shot at changing how we all behave and interact with humanity. And in the process, we might even learn something new.

THANKS

First off, I want to thank *you.*

Thank you for taking the time out of your life to read this book. I have so much gratitude for everyone who helped me through this journey and stuck around to watch it all unfold. All the blood, sweat, and tears that have gone into this book has made me a better man today, and it wouldn't have been possible without the love and support from so many people.

Huge thanks to my friend, writing coach, and publisher, Samantha Joy. Without her guidance and help with this process, you wouldn't be reading this book today. She helped me bring my story and vision to life. I am forever grateful for her support.

I want to thank Julia, Zora, and Publishizer for their crowdfunding efforts to get this book off the ground and for their guidance through my roadblocks.

Thank you to all of you who supported the crowdfunding campaign, including my sponsors, Balazs W. Kardos, Jack and April Tu, Ronny Turiaf, and Jesse Dylan.

Thank you to Paul and Matt for lending their artistic genius to create a powerful cover and brand for the book and to all my team members past and present for their hard work in getting me to where I am today.

I want to give special thanks to one of my oldest friends, Balazs W. Kardos, who became a mentor of mine and encouraged me to make a change in my life to get out of the bar and into a new life. He helped me learn the skills I needed to be able to think differently and move forward into a new direction in my life.

Thank you to my mom and my brother Aaron, for always encouraging me. And thanks to all the rest of my family and friends, who have believed in me and my vision and have given endless support from day one.

ABOUT LANCE ESSIHOS

Lance Essihos, a Canada native and world traveler, has made it his life's mission to help heal the world through the art of powerful storytelling and human connection. He is the host of the top-rated podcast *University of Adversity*, motivating hundreds of thousands of listeners to turn their darkest days into their greatest motivators. He has interviewed over 350 renowned people all over the globe, including world-class entrepreneurs, pro athletes, celebrities, doctors, spiritual masters, and the common heroes among us.

Lance is also the Founder & CEO of Mic-Up Media, an agency that helps founders and visionary leaders grow their businesses, brands, and networks through podcasting.

Learn more about Lance's journey, listen to his Top-Rated podcast, *University of Adversity*, and stay informed on upcoming programs at:

LanceEssihos.com